CULTURAL PERSPECTIVES IN STUDENT AFFAIRS WORK

CULTURAL PERSPECTIVES IN STUDENT AFFAIRS WORK

George D. Kuh
Editor

American College Personnel Association

Distributed by
University Press of America

4720 Boston Way
Lanham, Maryland 20706

3 Henrietta Street
London WC2E 8LU England

Library of Congress Cataloging-in-Publication Data

Cultural perspectives in student affairs work /
George D. Kuh, editor.
p.   cm.
Includes bibliographical references.
1. Student affairs services—Social aspects—United States.
2. College students—United States—Social life and customs.
I. Kuh, George D.
LB2342.9.D83   1993   378.1'94—dc20   93–3915 CIP

ISBN 1–883485–00–2 (cloth : alk. paper)
ISBN 1–883485–01–0 (pbk. : alk. paper)

 The paper used in this publication meets the minimum requirements of
American National Standard for Information Sciences—Permanence
of Paper for Printed Library Materials, ANSI Z39.48–1984.

Contents

Preface

In the summer of 1989, students in my doctoral seminar on college and university cultures at Indiana University made some pithy observations about the student affairs literature. Why, they wondered, were there so few published papers that addressed the influence of culture on student behavior?

In the 1950s and 1960s papers focusing on such aspects of culture as institutional mission and student subcultures were relatively common. In the 1970s and early 1980s, cultural perspectives were used less frequently. Within the past decade, however, cultural perspectives have been used more frequently to examine behavior in colleges and universities (Chaffee & Tierney, 1988; Kuh & Whitt, 1988). Yet, except for a handful of books (e.g., Horowitz, 1987; Moffatt, 1989), the literature has been essentially silent with regard to the influence of institutional culture on student behavior.

Also during the summer of 1989, Ernie Pascarella and Pat Terenzini shared with me some emerging findings from their synthesis of the research of the impact of college on students. Their excellent book, *How College Affects Students* (Pascarella & Terenzini, 1991), coupled with my own research on "Involving Colleges" (Kuh, Schuh, Whitt, Andreas, Lyons, Strange, Krehbiel and MacKay, 1991), pointed to the important influence of a college's environmental and contextual conditions (e.g., institutional culture) on student learning and personal development. Taken together, these observations suggested that the time was ripe for a volume that specifically addressed properties of college and university cultures with which student affairs practitioners should be familiar.

Purpose

The purpose of this book is to describe how student affairs professionals can use cultural perspectives in their work. Toward this end, the contributors emphasize implications and applications of cultural perspectives by drawing on reviews of the literature and their experience in different kinds of colleges and universities. The book is intended to assist new and continuing staff members in identifying, understanding, and appreciating the influence of institutional culture on the behavior of students, faculty, and staff. It also can be used as a reference when developing and evaluating student affairs programs and services.

OVERVIEW OF CHAPTERS

In the first chapter, George Kuh and Jenness Hall define culture as the term is used in this book and present a framework that student affairs professionals can use to examine cultural phenomena. Also, Kuh and Hall discuss characteristics of collegiate cultures that explain why "simple" approaches to "manage" or control culture inevitably fail.

In Chapter 2, Kathleen Manning describes in detail some of the more important properties of institutional culture introduced in Chapter 1. Particular attention is given to institutional traditions, normative behaviors, and language as well as the influence of institutional values and assumptions about teaching and learning on student behavior.

In Chapter 3, Patrick Love, George Kuh, Kathleen MacKay, and Christine Hardy compare the "cultures" of academic and student affairs. They contrast assumptions undergirding faculty culture(s) with assumptions and beliefs common to student affairs distilled from some of the basic documents of the field. The implications of espoused and enacted assumptions held by faculty members and student affairs professionals are discussed.

Student subcultures are addressed in Chapter 4 by Patrick Love, Bruce Jacobs, Vic Boschini, Christine Hardy, and George Kuh. Attention is given to the various types of student subcultures that typically exist on college campuses, how subcultures form, the functions they play in the institution, and implications for working with student groups.

In Chapter 5, Elizabeth Whitt describes a strategy for discovering the influence of culture on student behavior. Such a discovery process is essential because the properties of institutional culture are usually tacit or taken for granted by members of the culture.

Emphasis is given to the use of qualitative methods for identifying how culture influences student behavior.

Once one understands the culture of a campus, then what? In Chapter 6, Shevawn Eaton and Kathleen Manning offer suggestions for purposefully influencing institutional culture and student subcultures.

Each of the preceding chapters concludes with activities that student affairs staff members can use to learn more about how the respective issues apply to their own campus. In the final chapter, Kuh offers some additional suggestions for incorporating cultural perspectives in the day-to-day work of student affairs professionals.

Acknowledgements

Putting together a book requires the patience and good will of many people. The ACPA Media Board was supportive throughout. The project began when John Schuh was Media Board Editor, and has been sustained through the good efforts of the current editor, Harold Cheatham. Harold and reviewers from the ACPA Media Board made many helpful suggestions for which I and the other contributors are grateful. Joyce Regester did her usual superb job translating my poor penmanship and incoherent dictation into something at least readable. Finally, thanks are due also to those students, past and present, who continually challenge me to think more clearly about aspects of college and university culture. I hope that they and my colleagues who work with faculty, staff, and undergraduates at institutions of higher education across the country will find this book instructive.

George D. Kuh
Bloomington, Indiana

REFERENCES

Chaffee, E.E., & Tierney, W.G. (1988). *Collegiate culture and leadership strategy.* New York: American Council on Education and Macmillan.

Horowitz, H.L. (1987). *Campus life: Undergraduate cultures from the end of the eighteenth century to the present.* New York: Knopf.

Kuh, G.D., Schuh, J.H., Whitt, E.J., Andreas, R.E., Lyons, J.W., Strange, C.C., Krehbiel, L.E., & MacKay, K.A. (1991). *Involving colleges: Successful approaches to fostering student learning and personal development outside the classroom.* San Francisco: Jossey-Bass.

Kuh, G.D., & Whitt, E.J. (1988). *The invisible tapestry: Culture in American colleges and universities.* ASHE-ERIC Higher Education Report, No. 1. Washington, D.C.: Association for the Study of Higher Education.

Moffatt, M. (1989). *Coming of age in New Jersey: College and American culture.* New Brunswick, NJ: Rutgers University Press.

Pascarella, E.T., & Terenzini, P.T. (1991). *How college affects students.* San Francisco: Jossey-Bass.

Contributors

Victor J. Boschini is Dean of Students at Butler University. He received the B.A. in political science and history from Mount Union College, the M.A. in college student personnel from Bowling Green State University, and the Ed.D. from Indiana University in higher education. Previously, he worked in student activities at Indiana University and DePauw University.

Shevawn Bogdan Eaton is a Ph.D. candidate at Indiana University with a major in higher education and a minor in public policy analysis. She received her B.S. in biology and M.S. in counseling and personnel services from Purdue University. She has worked in residence life at Ball State University and the University of Dayton.

Jenness E. Hall is a Ph.D. candidate at Indiana University with a major in higher education and a minor in American history. She received her B.A. in English and history from Berry College in Rome, Georgia, and M.A. in college student personnel from Bowling Green State University. Jenness worked in student affairs, primarily residence life, at the College of Notre Dame (MD).

Christine M. Hardy is currently a Ph.D. candidate at Indiana University majoring in higher education with a minor in law. She received her B.A. in mass communications from the University of Denver and M.Ed. in college student personnel from Colorado State University. She worked in orientation at Colorado State University and with fraternities and sororities at Hartwick College.

Bruce A. Jacobs is Assistant Dean of Students and Director of Residence Life at Indiana University. He has a B.S. in political science and M.Ed. in educational administration from the State University of New York at Brockport. Formally Assistant Dean of

Residence Life at Rutgers College, he is completing his doctorate in higher education at Indiana University.

George D. Kuh is professor of higher education at Indiana University. He has the B.A. in English and history from Luther College, M.S. in counseling from St. Cloud State University, and Ph.D. in counselor education and higher education from the University of Iowa. Currently affiliated with the Center for Postsecondary Research and Planning at Indiana University, he has worked in admissions and placement and served in several administrative positions including Associate Dean for Academic Affairs in the Indiana University School of Education.

Patrick G. Love is assistant professor of higher education at Syracuse University. He received both his B.A. in political science and his M.A./C.A.S. in counseling psychology and student personnel from the State University of New York at Albany. His Ph.D. in higher education and educational inquiry is from Indiana University. Love has worked in residence life at LeMoyne College, SUNY-Stony Brook, and SUNY-Albany.

Kathleen A. MacKay is currently teaching in the higher education and student affairs program at Indiana University. She received her B.A. in journalism from Colorado State University, M.S. in college student personnel administration from the University of Vermont, and Ph.D. in higher education and sociology from Indiana University. MacKay has worked in student affairs at Michigan State University and Mills College.

Kathleen Manning is assistant professor of higher education and student affairs at the University of Vermont. She has a B.S. in biology from Marist College (NY), M.A. in counseling and student personnel from the State University of New York at Albany, and Ph.D. in higher education and anthropology from Indiana University. Manning has worked in various student affairs positions at Curry College, Emerson College, and Trenton State College.

Elizabeth J. Whitt is assistant professor of higher education at Iowa State University. She received her B.A. in history from Drake University, M.A. in college student personnel administration from Michigan State University, and Ph.D. in higher education and sociology from Indiana University. Previously on the faculty at Oklahoma State University, Whitt has worked in residence life and was dean of students at Doane College.

CHAPTER 1

Cultural Perspectives
in Student Affairs

George D. Kuh
Jenness E. Hall

What do the following situations have in common?

A college president laments what seems to be an erosion of the sense of community which used to characterize her campus.

Despite the change in legal drinking age to 21, numerous alcohol education programs, and more rigorous enforcement of campus alcohol policies, many students continue to engage in hazardous use of alcohol.

A residence hall annually shows X-rated films that demean women.

Although a desire to attract and graduate students from historically underrepresented groups is often espoused, the campus climate remains chilly and inhospitable for persons of color and women.

At a large research university, student affairs staff members feel estranged from and unappreciated by the faculty.

The above scenarios have several things in common. First, they describe issues common to most colleges and universities in the United States. Second, efforts to deal with these issues have been ineffective because they have not taken into account the dynamic interplay among institutional conditions, and the social, political and economic forces that influence the campus environment. Third, the issues represent *cultural phenomena* in that the behaviors exhibited in each situation are products of the confluence of institutional history, campus traditions, and the values and assumptions

1

that shape the character of a given college or university. So it follows that when examining the issues that affect a particular academic community, an institution's cultural aspects must be addressed.

In this chapter, culture is defined and a framework is presented to identify key cultural properties. The influence of culture on various aspects of institutional life is considered and the disciplinary roots of cultural perspectives are briefly summarized.

TOWARD A DEFINITION OF CULTURE

Alaskan Indians have about a dozen words for snow. Similarly, people who study and think about organizational culture have different meanings for the concept of culture (Frost, Moore, Louis, Lundberg & Martin, 1985). Indeed, scores of definitions of culture have been proposed (Kuh & Whitt, 1988).

The American Heritage Dictionary defines culture as "the totality of socially transmitted behavior patterns, arts, beliefs, institutions, and all other products of human work and thought characteristic of a community or population; a style of social and artistic expression peculiar to a society or class." Allaire and Firsirotu (1984) define culture as a system that embodies an institution's expressive and affective dimensions through shared symbols, ideology, values, myths, rites, rituals, customs, language, sagas, stories, legends, institutional logos, design and architecture.

Some advocate a functional view of culture wherein a group of people develop "a set of solutions . . . to meet specific problems posed by the situations they face in common" (Van Maanen & Barley, 1985, p. 31). Others view cultures as social constructions and emphasize the meanings people give to objects, events and actions, interpretations which are so pervasive that they become "reality" to the members of the culture (Berger & Luckmann, 1966).

In this book, culture is viewed as the collective, mutually shaping patterns of institutional history, mission, physical settings, norms, traditions, values, practices, beliefs and assumptions which guide the behavior of individuals and groups in an institution of higher education and which provide frames of reference for interpreting the meanings of events and actions on and off campus. This definition has utility for student affairs professionals for three reasons. First, it acknowledges the complexity and variety inherent in higher education by emphasizing the influence of such factors as an institution's mission and educational purposes, physical attributes, established practices, celebratory events, and symbols and symbolic actions. Second, the definition recognizes that while an institution may have a unifying system of beliefs and practices, distinct groups and subcultures, each with their own beliefs and practices, also may exist in the institution. For example, Greek organizations, honors students, athletes, and members of racial and ethnic groups may each have distinctive interaction patterns and norms that influence expectations for how people relate to each other. Finally, the definition acknowledges that institutional history and traditions as well as changes in the external environment and characteristics of students influence a college's culture and subcultures.

What Culture Is and Does

Just as there are many ways of defining culture, so too are there different views of what culture is and does. Some suggest the concept of culture is best used as a metaphor; that is, a college is *like* a culture (Morgan, 1986). In this sense, culture can be used as an analytical lens to identify the institutional attributes that provide behavioral cues in the institutional context. Others believe that culture is something a college *is* (Frost, Moore, Louis, Lundberg & Martin, 1985; Peterson, Cameron, Mets, Jones & Ettington, 1986). In this view, culture can be thought of as an independent variable which influences such behavioral outcomes as student performance and satisfaction reflected in retention rates as well as overall institutional effectiveness indicated by fiscal stability. At the same time, campus culture can be the dependent variable; that is, a product of the characteristics, attitudes, and behavior of faculty, staff, and students and the external environment. Because an institution's culture is both cause and effect, a college simultaneously exerts an influence on the behavior of students, faculty and staff while these same persons influence and define the institution's culture.

The simultaneous and mutually shaping qualities of cultural properties explain, in part, why institutional cultures are relatively stable but not stagnant; that is, change occurs over time as the attitudes, values and behaviors of people moving in and out of the setting interact with the structural elements of the institution and the ex-

ternal environment. So although collegiate cultures appear to be
stable in the short term, they change over time, influenced by such
external forces as shifting demographics, cataclysmic events (e.g.,
destruction of facilities or accidents that take the lives of senior
administrators or athletic teams—Peterson et al., 1986), or the presence of people whose beliefs and assumptions differ from those
held by the majority.

Levels of Culture

To understand the complex interplay of the myriad properties
that work together to create a cultural milieu, four levels of culture
have been identified: (a) artifacts, (b) perspectives, (c) values, and
(d) assumptions (Dyer, 1986; Lundberg, 1985; Schein, 1985).

Artifacts are the tangible aspects of culture, the meaning and
functions of which may be known by members. Physical, verbal,
and behavioral artifacts are described in this section.

Physical artifacts are "those things that surround people physically and provide them with immediate sensory stimuli as they carry
out culturally expressive activities" (Kuh & Whitt, 1988, p. 19).
They include technology, indoor and outdoor spaces, art, and architecture. An institution's physical setting, including permanent
structures, land as well as the region of the country where a college or university is located, shape its culture.

For example, the Quad at Stanford University, the campus green
at the University of Virginia, Sproull Plaza at the University of
California, Berkeley, the Yard at Harvard University, and the Golden
Dome at the University of Notre Dame are physical attributes that
set these institutions apart. The use of green space, and its symbolic importance, can create a sense of specialness among students
and faculty. The Heart at Earlham College is a grassy area near the
center of campus surrounded by a sidewalk. This area is called the
Heart for two reasons: (a) this location allows one to see virtually
all the buildings on the Earlham campus, and (b) this is the location for "vigils," those occasions when the Earlham community
comes together to reflect on important social, political or moral
issues facing the world and the campus community (Krehbiel &
Strange, 1991). When urban universities preserve green space and
expose students to fine art through outdoor sculptures (as does
Wichita State University), they send powerful messages to exter-

nal audiences as well as students, faculty and staff about how the institution differs from the surrounding urban area and they encourage people to behave differently, in ways consistent with the institution's values and expectations (Kuh, Schuh, Whitt & Associates, 1991).

Language, stories, and myths are examples of *verbal* artifacts. Becker and Geer (1970) observed that:

> "Any social group, to the extent that it is a distinctive unit, will have to some degree . . . a language whose nuances are peculiar to that group. Members of churches speak differently from members of tavern groups; more importantly, members of any particular church or tavern group have cultures, and languages in which they are expressed, which differs somewhat from those of other groups of the same general type" (p. 134).

"Terms of endearment" are institution-specific words and phrases commonly used by students, faculty, staff and graduates (Kuh et al., 1991). At the University of Massachusetts at Amherst, the phrase "oppression education" connotes the institution's commitment to eradicate various forms of "isms" (e.g., racism and sexism). At Stanford University, "running the dish" means jogging into the foothills near the edge of the 8,000+ acre campus where a communications transmitter and receiver are located (Kuh, 1991). Knowing the meaning of terms of endearment in the context of a particular campus differentiates insiders from outsiders. Also, the meaning of language gives clues to newcomers about how to behave and what is valued.

Behavioral artifacts are represented by rituals and ceremonies. Rites, rituals and other celebratory events translate culture into action and connect the past to the present (Masland, 1985). Mount Holyoke College, for example, has traditions such as "milk and crackers" (a study break in the evenings) and the Laurel Chain at graduation which symbolically connects alumna with current students (Whitt, 1991). While certain rituals may not be particularly distinctive, they can be, nonetheless, important vehicles by which an institution expresses its values: awards for student and staff achievements; public acknowledgements for noteworthy performance; banquets, retreats, and other gatherings that denote beginnings (e.g., orientation) and endings (e.g., commencement); informal meetings and coffee breaks; and celebrations (Kuh, Whitt &

Shedd, 1987). Miami University of Ohio, for example, invites people from the local community to nominate students who have performed outstanding public service and to join their nominee at a spring award banquet.

Perspectives are the socially shared rules and norms applicable to a given context. In essence, perspectives are "the way we do things here" and define and determine what is "acceptable behavior" for students, faculty, staff and others in various institutional settings. They are relatively easy to determine and the members of various groups who adhere to perspectives are usually aware of them. Another way of thinking about perspectives is that they are social conventions manifested through behavior.

Artifacts such as the style of attire reflect the cultural perspectives of different groups. Fraternity members at Miami University and Indiana University, for example, commonly wear button-down collar shirts, khaki pants and penny loafers suggesting the importance of tradition and collegiate life. At The Evergreen State College and Grinnell College, the style of dress is much more casual, reflecting the egalitarian ethos of their colleges. Other examples of perspectives are the periods of silence before speaking at the beginning of discussions at Earlham, a Quaker custom (Krehbiel & Strange, 1991), secret ballot voting in faculty meetings (as contrasted with voice-vote), and taboos that prohibit public discussions of sexual orientations other than heterosexual at many small colleges and in most male fraternities.

Values reflect the espoused as well as the enacted ideals of an institution or group and serve as the basis on which members of a culture or subculture judge situations, acts, objects and people. Values are more abstract than perspectives although long-time members of a culture (e.g., senior faculty and administrators) are able to articulate them in ways that are more or less compatible with statements of institutional philosophy and mission. Moreover, the mission and philosophy of the institution both shape, and are shaped by, the culture. That is, what institutional leaders say the institution aspires to be coupled with the expectations constituents both on and off the campus have for the institution determine the institution's *living* mission; the living mission may or may not be congruent with the published mission statement.

Berea College emphasizes the value of work in its written mission and philosophy. One of the Seven Great Commitments, the guiding principles of Berea, is focused on labor. Everyone works, no student whose family can contribute more than $2300 per year can attend Berea. At Earlham College, Grinnell College, and The Evergreen State University, egalitarian values dominate; at Miami University and Xavier University in New Orleans, meritocratic values are ingrained. As a result, these values influence how people are addressed and how teaching and learning take place.

Values may be espoused and enacted. Espoused values take the form of assertions about such institutional aspirations as expecting students to be responsible for their own behavior or embracing diversity; college catalogs and speeches by institutional leaders commonly espouse values to which the institution aspires. Espoused values, however, may not reflect the experiences of all members of the community (e.g., students are told what to do, people of color feel alienated). Enacted values are those that guide policy, decisionmaking, and other practices. For example, in research universities, research and publications commonly receive more weight in institutional reward systems. This enacted value (the importance of research) may contradict the espoused importance of undergraduate teaching frequently mentioned in public statements. Conflictual values also operate in student affairs; for example, although most institutions assert that they wish their students to become independent thinkers and challenge unjust policies and practices, when students protest against campus policies, institutions often move to discourage such actions.

Assumptions are the tacit beliefs that members use to define their role, their relationships to others, and the nature of the organization in which they live. In this sense, they are implicit, abstract axioms on which artifacts, perspectives, and values are based. Faculty, student affairs staff, and students typically are not aware of their shared assumptions and beliefs; they are so familiar they are taken for granted and exist as tacit knowledge. Schein (1985) suggested that while assumptions are relatively few in number, the substance of the assumptions differs from one culture to another. Schein identified five core assumptions (p. 86). They are:

(a) Humanity's relationship to nature. For example, how do faculty leaders, senior administrators, and heroes and heroines in the student cultures view the relationship of the institution to its environment? Is the relationship viewed as dominant, harmonious, or submissive? At The Evergreen State University, the institution's relationship to the environment is harmonious. Evergreen's proximity to Puget Sound coupled with a keen interest in ecological issues calls for environmentally responsible behavior, such as recycling and use of biodegradable materials (Lyons, 1991);

(b) The nature of reality and truth including the linguistic and behavioral rules or perspectives that define what is real and what is not, what is a "fact," how truth is ultimately to be determined, and whether truth is revealed or discovered. At Earlham College, it is assumed that the "light of truth" cannot not be found in any one individual or discipline. This accounts for Earlham's emphasis on collaboration and multidisciplinary learning (Krehbiel & Strange, 1991);

(c) The nature of human nature itself—what it means to be "human" and what attributes are considered intrinsic or ultimate? Is human nature good, evil or neutral? Are human beings perfectible (educable) or not? At some colleges, such as Xavier University of New Orleans, it is assumed that anyone can learn anything, given the right circumstances (Andreas, 1991). Therefore, complementary policies and programs have been developed to assist students in acquiring the skills needed to be successful;

(d) The nature of human activities such as what constitutes appropriate behavior in the institutional context consistent with the assumptions related to the natural environment, reality, and human nature. That is, are people to be active, passive, independent and autonomous, interdependent, or fatalistic? What is considered work and what is considered play and what is the proper balance? For example, Grinnell college, Stanford University, and Earlham College expect students to be responsible for their own learning and social behavior. At Grinnell, this expectation is manifested by requiring only one course; therefore, students must exercise independent judgment in planning their program of study (Kuh et al., 1991); and

(e) The nature of human relations or the "right" way for people to relate to each other. Is institutional life cooperative or competitive, individualistic or collaborative and communal, based on traditional lineal authority, law, or charisma? We have already alluded to institutions where cooperation and collaboration are expected (e.g., Earlham, Evergreen State); at other colleges, such as Reed College, individualistic approaches to learning are emphasized. Some universities have a corporate ethos where deference to authority is expected (Kuh, in press).

It is important to note that the assumptions which undergird an institution's values, perspectives and artifacts are not necessarily good or bad. Nor are some assumptions necessarily better for promoting student learning and development. Whether students act responsibly and take advantage of learning opportunities depends on many context-specific conditions and factors, not the least of which is the degree to which student characteristics and expectations are congruent with the institution's expectations.

HOW CULTURES ARE CREATED

Cultures are created overtime as people convene regularly, talk, and do things over and over again. Clearly, colleges and universities are "culture-bearing milieus" (Louis, 1985); they are organized to encourage continuing interactions among groups of people that generate opportunities for affiliation. Settings such as residence halls, the campus union, and academic departments, and structures such as governance bodies and curriculum committees direct the attention of certain groups of people to certain issues and away from others. In the process, interdependent relationships evolve as people do things for themselves, for others, and for the institution. These relationships contribute to shared understandings as well as a sense of specialness and identity for members—what they stand for, and how they deal with one another and with outsiders (Louis, 1983, 1985). Over time, such interactions foster feelings of belonging and shared assumptions that engender trust and loyalty, attributes that perpetuate an institution's special, distinctive qualities (Clark, 1972). Loyalty keeps such groups as graduates and senior faculty and staff connected to the institution; in strong cultures, these emotional bonds run deep and promote a sense or feeling of community. Hence, when described in terms of shared patterns of beliefs, meanings, rituals, symbols and other properties that evolve across time, an institution's culture is the "social glue" that keeps the organization together (Smircich, 1983).

Subcultures

Colleges and universities encompass many groups (faculty, students, administrators, staff members, graduates and so on) with different and often competing interests which create "a mosaic of organizational realities rather than a uniform corporate culture" (Morgan, 1986, p. 127). So rarely does a single institutional culture dominate. The student culture—which at first glance appears to be monolithic—is, upon examination, composed of disparate subgroups (Clark & Trow, 1966; Kuh 1990).

Subcultures are "distinctive social units possessed of a set of common understandings for organizing action (e.g., what we are doing together in this particular group, appropriate ways of doing in and among members of the group) and languages and other symbolic vehicles for expressing common understandings" (Louis, 1983, p. 39). The language members of subcultures use to communicate with each other, and to refer to other groups, sets one's group apart from other groups. For example, fraternities are status-driven organizations (Kuh & Lyons, 1990); the very act of joining a group with restrictive entrance standards creates a "we-they" relationship that is difficult to avoid. In describing his group, one fraternity leader said, "We are no different from *'ordinary'* students." Using the term "ordinary" to describe other students implied that membership in his group did, indeed, make one different than others. In this way, culture can be thought of as "a set of blinders limiting the alternatives that individuals perceive, as well as the variables with which they must deal" (Krefting & Frost, 1985, p. 156).

Subcultures exist within the administration and faculty as well. Evidence that student affairs may be a subculture of administrative staff can be found by examining departmental slogans such as "students are our business" signs, "do it in the halls" staff t-shirts, and "I care about student success" buttons. As with student subcultures, a student affairs division can have its own heroines and heroes who personify ideals and values. They may be nationally known pioneers in the student affairs field, articulate spokespersons for the contributions of student services to the quality of campus life, charismatic leaders such as a longtime dean of students, or unusually creative thinkers such as the architect of an innovative alcohol education program or a resident assistant (RA) who successfully coped with a student in crisis (Kuh et al., 1987). Differences between the cultures of student affairs and faculty are addressed in more detail in Chapter 3.

Culture as a Socializing Agent

The institutional culture and its subcultures are the primary vehicles through which newcomers are taught how to behave and what is valued by their institution. In most colleges, at least 30% of the students are new each year. Consider the influence of the student culture on new students who arrive at college with a heightened sense of anticipation and high expectations for teaching and learning. Within a few weeks, newcomers receive messages from the student culture about the degree of effort that is needed to "get by." The following variables work together in context- specific ways to shape student behavior: patterns of eating, sleeping, studying and socializing; tacit understandings about what activities on campus are status enhancing or status degrading; the norms determining acceptable behavior in and out of the classroom; the student grapevine that tells students what classes are "gut," and which are challenging, and professors from whom to take classes and those to avoid. "In brief, student cultures offer their members thick and thin guidelines for how to get an education and thus define for students just what an education means" (Van Maanen, 1987, p. 5). So student culture redefines for new students the role of faculty, their accessibility and expectations for students (Becker & Geer, 1970).

"Chains of socialization" (Van Maanen, 1984) shape the student affairs professional's expectations and assumptions about higher education, student affairs work, and teaching and learning. "Links" in a socialization chain include undergraduate and graduate school experiences including major field and participation in organizations and leadership positions, the transition from graduate school to the job setting, and taking a position at a new institution. These experiences determine, in part, how people learn to act toward one another and what to expect and to do under certain circumstances (Van Maanen, 1984).

Anticipatory socialization is the process by which people begin to adopt the perspectives of the groups with which they wish to affiliate. Through anticipatory socialization experiences (e.g., graduate school), student affairs staff members are introduced to the cultural properties that warrant attention. But people also carry culture with them. "Leaving one setting for another does not mean that the cultural premises of the first are abandoned for those of the second" (Van Maanen, 1984, p. 217). Newcomers must be prepared to shed expectations acquired from their "culture of orientation" (previous places of employment or educational preparation) where one was first introduced to ways of knowing and acting that are supposed to useful in the present setting and learn what is required to be successful in their "culture of employment" (where one now works and lives). The cultural properties (e.g., artifacts, perspectives, values, assumptions) of one's culture of employment may differ—in some cases markedly—from one's culture of orientation and result in culture shock and frustration in the first few weeks and months on the job.

ORIGINS OF THE CULTURAL PERSPECTIVE

Cultural perspectives provide an integrative view of institutional life because they draw on such disciplines as psychology, sociology, anthropology, social psychology, organizational behavior, and psychotherapy (Schein, 1985). While it is beyond the scope of this presentation to examine these views in-depth, a brief overview of the contributions of sociology, psychology, and anthropology is presented for those considering further reading in this area.

Sociology, the study of group behavior, emphasizes aggregated features of a group of people and the group's symbolic devices, such as myths and language, that convey group ideals. At the same time, people define situations, assess what is relevant, and determine how individuals and groups will respond based on their preferred interpretations of what is going on using previous experiences from different cultures (Schutz, 1967). For this reason, knowledge of psychology, the study of individual behavior, contributes to an understanding of culture because "individuals act toward things on the basis of the meanings that the things have for them" (Blumer, 1969, p. 2): that is, how an individual responds in any given situation is determined by that person's interpretation of what is going on.

While sociology and psychology are foundations of cultural perspectives, other disciplines, particularly anthropology, have contributed significantly to understanding college and university life. Anthropology is divided into schools of thought. For illustrative purposes, four approaches to the study of culture from anthropology are presented: functionalist, interpretive, radical humanist, and radical structuralist.

The *functionalist* view (Malinowski, 1953) is based on five axioms. Culture is: (a) a framework to deal with problems and satisfy needs; (b) a system of objects, activities, and attitudes that are a means to an end (e.g., survival), (c) a social system with interdependent elements; (d) an infrastructure that links the economic, political, legal, or educational activities of families, clans, communities, colleges and student affairs divisions; and (e) a network of shared beliefs which shape behavior such as a professional codes of ethics. This view assumes that most, if not all, of an institution's cultural properties are interrelated and exist to meet the needs of individuals and contribute to the survival of the group in its environment (Homans, 1950). In this sense, a college or university can be thought of as a miniature society with its own distinctive social structure, action patterns, language, discourse, roles, rituals, customs, ceremonies, norms, folklore, stories, beliefs, and myths (Morgan, Frost & Pondy, 1983). By thinking of a college or student affairs division as a culture, administrators are reminded to attend to behavior that is not accounted for by the formal administrative structure, such as reporting lines delineated in the organizational chart or activities listed in job descriptions.

From an *interpretive* view, culture attempts to understand the processes and practices by which cultural elements are created and sustained and people give meaning to events, actions and behavior (Morgan et al., 1983). That is, an interpretive approach underscores how individuals define and make sense of events and actions in the institutional setting that, over time, are interpreted in similar ways. The interpretive perspective attempts "to understand how the objective, taken for granted aspects of daily life are constituted and made real through the medium of symbolic processes" (Morgan et al., 1983, p. 22). For example, one might think of campus life as a living manuscript or "text" through which the interactions among faculty and students are living characters. The challenge is to understand the meaning of the interactions between the characters. By using the specific rules and conventions on which language is based within the text (campus), one can observe and analyze interactions to determine significant patterns of meaning within the historical and current context of a particular campus. Thus, the interpretive perspective emphasizes how symbolic activity creates and sustains distinctive patterns in campus life (Morgan et al., 1983).

A *radical humanist* approach to culture assumes that people create and sustain a world that has alienating properties for certain groups. Morgan (1986) suggested that colleges and universities can be thought of as "psychic prisons" because the institution channels behavior, events and actions according to perceived survival needs. From this view, faculty and students may exhibit blind allegiance to socially created rules and mores that over time are viewed as imperatives. Hence, patterns of institutional life may have deep structural significance (Morgan et al., 1983). The psychic prison analogy has been applied to individuals as well. For example, Jung's (1923) concept of the "archetype" is an undergirding premise of instruments such as the *Myers-Briggs Type Indicator* (Myers & McCaulley, 1985). The archetype depicts unconscious tendencies or predispositions to behave in a certain way consistently over time. The radical humanist view may be useful for understanding why institutions of higher education continue to be perceived as non-affirming by such groups as African Americans and women.

The *radical structuralist* perspective suggests that colleges and universities dominate and oppress individuals by creating class and status structures that are manipulated and controlled by members of preferred classes (e.g., senior faculty lord over junior faculty, members of prestigious organizations such as fraternities or student government receive preferential treatment in housing or parking assignments). Hence, the institutional culture communicates a dominant social ideology that is controlled by those in power. In this view, it is possible to conclude that the cultures of many institutions of higher education are manipulated by white males.

Sociology, psychology, anthropology and other cultural perspectives (e.g., ecological-adaptionist and historical-diffusionist views— Allaire & Firsirotu, 1984) contribute to the variety of definitions of culture and remind us that there are many ways to view cultural phenomena; no one discipline is best because each has limitations depending on the issues one is attempting to understand. Taken together, however, they can generate multiple interpretations of how cultural properties influence behavior, and fuel the debate about whether it is possible to intentionally change or manipulate culture (Kuh & Whitt, 1988).

SUMMARY AND ACTIVITIES

Cultural perspectives can be used by student affairs professionals to understand their purpose and role in an institution of higher education and how meaning is made within an institutional context as well as at the level of various student affairs functional areas (e.g., residence life, discipline, student activities). The history of the institution, including the purposes for which it was founded and the aspirations of the founding body, is a legacy which shapes the present and future (Clark, 1970; Chaffee & Tierney, 1988; Frost et al., 1985; Kuh & Whitt, 1988). An awareness of the past is needed to understand the cycles of institutional life, such as the renewal of interest in fraternities and sororities as well as alcohol use as a behavioral manifestation of rebellion by students (Horowitz, 1987). Cultural perspectives also draw attention to some of the more subtle aspects of college and university life, such as the symbolic importance of rituals, myths, stories, and legends in interpreting events, ideas and experiences and why some practices in certain student cultures seem to be intractable.

Using cultural perspectives in student affairs work is a complex, challenging undertaking that requires an unusual blend of skills and attitudes as well as sensitivity, courage, and awareness. The sensitivities and inclinations of a therapist are helpful in probing and unraveling the implications and significance of cultural experiences. Krefting and Frost (1985) compared the administrator who uses cultural perspectives to "a wildcatter drilling the cultural terrain, to find and release hidden or blocked human resources" (p. 157).

While a good deal is known about institutional culture, some aspects of culture remain mysterious and other aspects elude consensus. For example, it is not always apparent how an institution's culture originates, whether a dominant institutional culture exists, if there are multiple layers of cultures, if cultures can be managed, or how and even *if* cultures should be studied at all. For the purposes of this volume, relatively little is known about many cultural features of college and university life in which student affairs professionals are interested. The chapters that follow address many of these features. In the next chapter, some of the more important properties of institutional culture are examined in more detail.

Activities

Before starting Chapter 2, we encourage the reader to engage in one or more of the following activities. These activities are designed to provide practice in applying the concepts introduced in this chapter.

(1) Review the formal written mission statement of your institu-

tion. How does the mission, as formally expressed, guide institutional decision-making and your own behavior? Does the written mission describe what actually takes place at the college? How does the president (or chief academic officer or chief student affairs officer) describe the institution's educational purposes and its philosophy? How do the espoused goals of the institution compare to what the institution actually does?

(2) Spend some time talking with one or more "institutional historians," people who have been long time employees and can provide a perspective of the history and traditions of the college. If possible, you might obtain different points of view by speaking with a faculty member, an administrator, and someone from the maintenance staff. Ask them to tell you the history of the institution and what makes it special.

(3) Try to see the institution's physical structures and use of space from a perspective other than your own. Take a walking tour of the campus, ideally with the institution's architect or with the campus historian. View the institution through the eyes of someone who may know why certain buildings and open spaces are placed where they are and how these facilities and spaces influence behavior.

(4) Take a tour of the campus led by an admissions officer and listen to how the institution is described to newcomers and note the reactions and questions of outsiders.

(5) Write out your own definition of institutional culture. Describe the most important elements of the culture of your institution. For example, what are your college's core values? Who are the heroic figures? What are some highly visible artifacts? You may wish to refer to this description as you engage in the activity suggested below and those offered in the remaining chapters.

(6) Consider how your institution's culture, as you have described it, is inclusive or exclusive of students, faculty and administrators from historically underrepresented groups. Does your institution's culture embrace multiculturalism as an important institutional aspiration? What aspects of your institution's culture need attention in order for your college to become more welcoming and affirming of members from historically underrepresented groups?

REFERENCES

Allaire, Y., & Firsirotu, M.E. (1984). Theories of organizational culture. *Organization Studies, 5*, 193-226.

Andreas, R.E. (1991). Where achievement is the rule: The case of Xavier University of Louisiana. In G. Kuh and J. Schuh (Eds.), *The role and contributions of student affairs in Involving Colleges* (pp. 97-114). Washington, D.C.: National Association of Student Personnel Administrators.

Astin, A.W. (1985). *Achieving educational excellence.* San Francisco: Jossey-Bass.

Berger, P.L., & Luckmann, T. (1966). *The social construction of reality.* Garden City, NY: Anchor.

Blumer, H. (1969). *Symbolic interactionism.* Englewood Cliffs, NJ: Prentice-Hall.

Chaffee, E.E., & Tierney, W.G. (1988). *Collegiate culture and leadership strategy.* New York: American Council on Education and Macmillan.

Clark, B.R. (1972). The organizational saga in higher education. *Administrative Science Quarterly, 17*(2), 178-184.

Clark, B.R., & Trow, M. (1966). The organizational context. In T.M. Newcomb and E.K. Wilson (Eds.), *College peer groups: Problems and prospects for research* (pp. 17-70). Chicago: Aldine.

Dyer, W.G., Jr. (1986). The cycle of cultural evolution in organizations. In R. Kilmann, M. Saxton, R. Serpa and Associates (Eds.), *Gaining control of the corporate culture* (pp. 200-229). San Francisco: Jossey-Bass.

Frost, P.J., Moore, L.F., Louis, M.R., Lundberg, C.C., & Martin, J. (1985). An allegorical view of organizational culture. In Frost, P.J., Moore, L.F., Louis, M.R., Lundberg, C.C., and Martin, J. (Eds.), *Organizational culture* (pp. 13-23). Beverly Hills, CA: Sage.

Homans, G.C. (1950). *The human group.* New York: Harcourt, Brace, World.

Horowitz, H.L. (1987). *Campus life: Undergraduate cultures from the end of the eighteenth century to the present.* New York: Knopf.

Jung, C.G. (1923). *Psychological types.* London: Routledge & Kegan Paul.

Krefting, L.A., & Frost, P.J. (1985). Untangling webs, surfing waves, and wildcatting: A multiple metaphor perspective on managing organizational culture. In P.J. Frost, L.F. Moore, M.R. Louis, C.C. Lundberg, and J. Martin (Eds.), *Organizational culture* (pp. 155-168). Beverly Hills, CA: Sage.

Krehbiel, L.E., & Strange, C.C. (1991). Checking of the truth: The case of Earlham College. In G. Kuh and J. Schuh (Eds.), *The role and contributions of student affairs in Involving Colleges* (pp. 148-167). Washington, D.C.: National Association of Student Personnel Administrators.

Kuh, G.D. (1990). Assessing student culture. In W. G. Tierney (Ed.), *Assessing academic climates and cultures, New Directions for Institutional Research*, No. 68 (pp. 47-60). San Francisco: Jossey-Bass.

Kuh, G.D. (1991). Caretakers of the collegiate culture: Student affairs at Stanford University. In G. Kuh and J. Schuh (Eds.), *The role and contributions of student affairs in Involving Colleges* (pp. 46-66). Washington, D.C.: National Association of Student Personnel Administrators.

Kuh, G.D. (in press). Appraising the character of a college. *Journal of Counseling and Development*.

Kuh, G.D., & Lyons, J.W. (1990). Greek systems at "involving colleges": Lessons from the College Experiences Study. *NASPA Journal, 28*, 20-29.

Kuh, G.D., Schuh, J.H., Whitt, E.J., Andreas, R.E., Lyons, J.W., Strange, C.C., Krehbiel, L.E., & MacKay, K.A. (1991). *Involving colleges: Successful approaches to fostering student learning and personal development outside the classroom*. San Francisco: Jossey-Bass.

Kuh, G.D., & Whitt, E.J. (1988). *The invisible tapestry: Culture in American colleges and universities*. ASHE-ERIC Higher Education, Report No. 1. Washington, D.C.: Association for the Study of Higher Education.

Kuh, G.D., Whitt, E.J., & Shedd, J. (1987). *Student affairs, 2001: A paradigmatic odyssey*. Alexandria, VA: American College Personnel Association.

Louis, M.R. (1983). Organizations as culture-bearing milieux. In L. R. Pondy, P. J. Frost, G. Morgan and T. C. Dandridge (Eds.), *Organizational symbolism* (pp. 39-54). Greenwich, CT: JAI.

Louis, M.R. (1985). An investigator's guide to workplace culture. In Frost, P.J., Moore, L.F., Louis, M.R., Lundberg, C.C., and Martin J. (Eds.), *Organizational culture* (pp. 73-93). Beverly Hills, CA: Sage.

Lundberg, C.C. (1985). On the feasibility of cultural intervention in organizations. In Frost, P.J., Moore, L.F., Louis, M.R., Lundberg, C.C., and Martin J. (Eds.), *Organizational culture* (pp. 169-186). Beverly Hills, CA: Sage.

Lyons, J.W. (1991). An eclipse of the usual: The Evergreen State College. In G. Kuh and J. Schuh (Eds.), *The role and contributions of student affairs in Involving Colleges* (pp. 173-198). Washington, D.C.: National Association of Student Personnel Administrators.

Malinowski, B. (1953). *Argonauts of the Western Pacific.* New York: Dutton.

Masland, A.T. (1985). Organizational culture in the study of higher education. *The Review of Higher Education, 8,* 157-168.

Morgan, G. (1986). *Images of organization.* Beverly Hills, CA: Sage.

Morgan, G., Frost, P. J., & Pondy, L. R. (1983). Organizational symbolism. In L. R. Pondy, P. J. Frost, G. Morgan and T. C. Dandridge (Eds.), *Organizational symbolism* (pp. 3-35). Greenwich, CT: JAI.

Myers, I.B., & McCaulley, M.H. (1985). *Manual for the Myers-Briggs Type Indicator: A Guide to the development and use of the MBTI.* Palo Alto, CA: Consulting Psychologists Press.

Peterson, M.W., Cameron, K.S., Mets, L.A., Jones, P., & Ettington, D. *The organizational context for teaching and learning: A review of the research literature.* Ann Arbor, MI: National Center for Research to Improve Postsecondary Teaching and Learning. (ED 287 437)

Schein, E.H. (1985). *Organizational culture and leadership.* San Francisco: Jossey-Bass.

Schutz, A. (1967). *The problem of social reality.* The Hauge: Martinus Nijhoff.

Smircich, L. (1983). Concepts of culture and organizational analysis. *Administrative Science Quarterly, 28,* 339-358.

Van Maanen, J. (1984). Doing old things in new ways: The chains of socialization. In J. Bess (Ed.), *College and university organization: Insights from the behavioral sciences* (pp. 211-247). New York: New York University Press.

Van Maanen, J. (1987, May). *Managing education better: Some thoughts on the management of student cultures in American colleges and universities.* Presented at the Meeting of the Association for Institutional Research, Kansas City.

Van Maanen, J., & Barley, S.R. (1985). Cultural organization: Fragments of a theory. In P.J. Frost, L.F. Moore, M.R. Louis, C.C. Lundberg, C.C., and J. Martin, (Eds.), *Organizational culture* (pp. 31-53). Beverly Hills, CA: Sage.

Whitt, E. J. (1991). A community of women empowering women: Mount Holyoke College. In G. Kuh and J. Schuh (Eds.), *The role and contributions of student affairs in Involving Colleges* (pp. 120-143). Washington, D.C.: National Association of Student Personnel Administrators.

CHAPTER 2

Properties of Institutional Culture

Kathleen Manning

As experts on students (Brown, 1972; National Association of Student Personnel Administrators, 1987), student affairs administrators use a variety of frameworks in order to understand and explain student behavior. By examining cultural properties of campus life, as suggested in Chapter 1, student affairs professionals will be better prepared to create the conditions that encourage students to take advantage of learning opportunities. This chapter explores how cultural properties (i.e., artifacts, perspectives, values, assumptions) work together to influence student behavior.

CULTURAL ARTIFACTS

As discussed in the preceding chapter, physical, verbal, and behavioral artifacts are the tangible properties of culture, the meaning and functions of which may or may not be immediately obvious to students, faculty, student affairs staff, or others. In this section, examples are offered of how the various forms of artifacts communicate the institution's mission and purposes and suggest to students the behaviors that are appropriate and those that are inappropriate.

Physical Cultural Artifacts

Written documents and publications, memorials, buildings, and campus grounds are examples of physical artifacts common to college campuses.

Documents. Yearbooks, handbooks, student newspapers, and memory books provide a wealth of information about a college's history, mission, and educational purposes. Old yearbooks chronicle the traditions that arise and disappear as well as the reasons for such turns of events. Student newspapers often provide excellent accounts of issues of interest to students. Past and present student publications can furnish student affairs professionals with insight into the gaps between formally espoused purposes (such as those contained in the catalog) and the enactment of those purposes (as evidenced in policies and practices as viewed through students' eyes).

Architecture and memorials. Campus grounds and architecture embody and reflect institutional history (Kuh & Whitt, 1988; Thelin & Yankovich, 1987). Residence halls reflect the au courrant architectural preferences of the period they were constructed (e.g., high rises in the 1960s) and priorities for student development (e.g., suites to create human scale, communal settings). Buildings named after campus founders and benefactors keep alive the aspirations and accomplishments of institutional heroes and heroines. The creation and maintenance of beautiful green spaces, quadrangles, and gathering places is testimony to an institution's commitment to promoting contemplation and thoughtful reflection.

The grave of Mary Lyon, the founder of Mount Holyoke College, is a strategically placed cultural stage on that campus. Stories about whether the founder *actually* is buried under the marker enhance the importance of the grave site to the college community. The controversy over whether she rests in the grave is important because her physical presence maintains the potency of the institution's founding values in contemporary times. The grave's central location on the campus as well as its role as a stage for college ceremonies (e.g., the trustees serve ice cream to students there at 6:00 a.m. on one Saturday each year) symbolically affirm important institutional values (e.g., students matter, the Founder's spirit remains alive) (Manning, 1989).

Sometimes physical structures communicate contradictory messages. The statue at the University of Vermont which memorializes Ira Allen, that institution's founder, is a reminder of both his tenacity as one of the state's early heroic figures as well as his unconscionable role as an "Indian killer." Understanding an individual's role (e.g., founder, distinguished graduate) communicates and clarifies institutional purposes while simultaneously contributing to a richer understanding of the campuses' history and values. Physical cultural artifacts are concrete reminders that the aspirations of institutional founders and the histories of their colleges often are inextricably intertwined.

Verbal Cultural Artifacts

Myths and stories passed on from one student cohort to the next carry messages year after year about what the institution values and expects of students and others. At colleges with strong cultures, prospective students hear about college traditions through stories told by paraprofessional admissions ambassadors and upperclass student leaders. Like it or not, stories and myths passed down from class to class, and the values transmitted through these verbal vehicles, are part and parcel of the undergraduate student culture on many campuses.

Sagas. Student organizations such as fraternities sustain their hegemony of hedonism and exclusivity (Maisel, 1990) through the use of sagas. A saga is "a collective understanding of a unique accomplishment in a formally established group. The group's definition of the accomplishment [is] intrinsically historical but [is] embellished through retelling and rewriting" (Clark, 1972, p. 178). However, the same kinds of myths and stories which build group and organizational solidarity sometimes endorse behavior that physically and emotionally threatens its members. Dangerous practices are inadvertently promoted when stories romanticize the camaraderie of a pledging activity, but minimize the risks of physical harm to self and others. The celebrative manner in which drinking episodes are retold is evidence of the power of such storytelling and mythmaking.

Campus language. Campus-specific language is another type of verbal artifact. Defining and describing a sense of place and belonging on campus, language has an affective component and can evoke emotional responses as stories are told and retold, elaborated and embellished (Fernandez, 1988). Influenced by the youth culture (Moffatt, 1989), the language of college students often is sprinkled with profanity and cohort-specific connotations borrowed from popular television programs and popular music. Words, phrases, and tonal intonation identify the speaker as a member of a particular ethnic group, residence hall, or social organization. Terms of endearment are created to refer to a specific places on a campus or in the local town and identify the speaker as a member of a particular institution or group (Kuh, Schuh, Whitt & Associates, 1991). For example, students at Syracuse University can be identified by their reference to "M Street"; the "M" stands for Marshall Street where bookstores, novelty shops, and drinking establishments frequented by students are located.

Behavioral Cultural Artifacts

Several categories of behavioral cultural artifacts are common to college campuses, including rituals, rites of passage, cultural performances, and traditions.

Rituals and rites of passage. Rituals and rites of passage performed by students, faculty, staff, and graduates differentiate a college as an educational institution from other human service agencies and organizations. Rituals, commonly called "rites of passage," are events "whose essential purpose is to enable the individual to pass from one defined position to another which is equally well-defined" (van Gennep, 1960, p. 3). Events to honor heroes and heroines, for example, can become rituals that provide opportunities to commemorate those who established the college. Founder's Day at Mount Holyoke College honors Mary Lyon, a pioneer of women's higher education. Another important ritual at Mount Holyoke is retracing Mary Lyon's well-documented trek through the neighboring countryside to collect pennies from supportive farm women (Manning, 1989).

Although a message communicated repeatedly over time can become firmly entrenched in campus lore, the meaning behind the activity and words of certain rituals is not always clear. Participation in convocations allow multiple interpretations of the ritual as college members make their own meaning of the event. The opening fall convocation is a time for faculty to affirm the academic mission of the college. For academic and student affairs administrators, the convocation can be used to articulate the college's aspirations and expectations for students. For students, it is a time to greet new friends, demonstrate school spirit, and have some fun.

The messages and meanings transmitted through rituals contribute to the long-term vitality of a college because of their ability to build consensus. Through the ritual itself, as well as conversation before, during, and after the events, college members forge common meanings with others (Kapferer, 1984). Individual interpretations of the ritual are shared and debated until common understandings are reached about "the way we do things around here." People who do not attend certain events often learn afterwards about the messages of the events, and interpret their meanings, through second-hand reports of the events as told by participants. Over time some of these stories evolve into campus sagas and myths. In this way, many college members vicariously experience the ritual's message. Certain rituals become more intriguing and more powerful as they are embellished by storytellers.

Cultural Performances. A college or university hosts many events that do not fit any of the formal definitions of rituals or rites of passage. Football games, community picnics, student talent shows, and memorial services do not qualify technically as rituals or rites of passage; yet these events are important manifestations cultural phenomena. Some cultural performances are more than entertainment, persuasive inventions, or cathartic indulgences. Evocative language often is used during cultural performances to solidify the bonds between students and the institution as well as to assert loyalty to the college and commitment to its purposes.

Some cultural performances are spontaneous and disorderly. Even so, they confer meaning (MacAloon, 1984) when they cause students, faculty, and administrators to reflect upon their role and more clearly define their purposes. Community soul searching by participants is sometimes required when cultural performances mark significant campus or global events. During these events, those in attendance examine alternatives to the definitions provided through speech and action and, eventually, may change in some ways and remain the same in others (MacAloon, 1984).

Cultural performances often embody conspicuous excesses, such as tinting hair or faces to match school colors, dressing as the school mascot, or shedding clothes. It is during cultural performances that humor, criticism, and even "sanctioned disrespect" (Babcock, 1984, p. 107) are expressed. For example, a throw-back to the "streaking" craze of the 1970s, the Cary Quad Nude Olympics at Purdue University is a cultural performance that started as a rebellious prank to express disdain for the conventional routines of campus life and the cold, harsh winters of West Lafayette, Indiana. Held at a reasonable hour after nightfall, the Olympics begin when people take off their clothes and run around the Cary Quad residence hall. In recent years university administrators have made it clear that the Nude Olympics violated campus policy; students, however, continue to take great delight in holding the spontaneous event all the same. Similar to Naked Softball at Grinnell College, participation in the Nude Olympics (either as a spectator or competitor) is a way for students to exercise independence and express impulse.

Cultural performances also provide opportunities for the institution to transcend the dichotomies of everyday campus living: public and private, practice and theory, doing and thinking, male and female, and college life and real world. Cultural events often serve this purpose by juxtaposing irreconcilable opposites in the same space: students exchange roles with administrators, men students dress in women's clothing, academicians take to the intramural basketball court. Because cultural performances usually are characterized by more spontaneity than a ritual or the well-practiced commentary of a myth or saga, observers exercise considerable latitude in interpreting the meaning of the event.

When a cultural event "fires" effectively (e.g., evokes emotions), a moment called "communitas" occurs. At some point an emotional peak is reached such that a "collective sentiment is created and accumulated in support of communal activity" (Lewis, 1980, p. 198). Although precariously fleeting due to its unplanned and spontaneous nature, the emotional wave of communitas can sweep through a crowd leaving an unmistakable impression on the participants. The feeling of "oneness" with other college members builds community in ways possible only during these communal events. The individual self is blended into the communal self. That is, an individual's history becomes part of the institution's communal history, and the communal history blends with the individual's history. As a result, an individual is connected to the campus, if only for brief periods of time (Burns & Laughlin, 1979). Thus, it is not surprising that college graduates often recall such events as among the best times they had in college (Manning, 1989).

Traditions

When trying to foster a sense of community on the contemporary college campus, administrators often hear the lament: "there aren't enough traditions at this institution." Examples of traditions include class colors, annual social events, expressions of school spirit, long-standing student organizations, and awards and leadership recognition ceremonies. The rallying cry for a return to tradition can be interpreted as a longing for the "good ol' days" when student aspirations and college expectations were clearer, shared purpose and common cause more easily achieved, and institutional values less conflictual. Another interpretation of these longings is a wish to return to the pre-1960s era when traditions were not considered as "corny" or "silly"; rather, they were events that instilled institutional pride and loyalty in students, faculty, student affairs staff, and others.

Multiculturalism. With increased student diversity and heightened awareness of cultural pluralism, the return to tradition necessitates the incorporation of more inclusive messages in these activities than was the case in the past. Traditions such as initiation of newcomers have historically discouraged, and in some instances excluded, women and people of color from participating in campus activities, holding leadership positions in governance committees, and becoming a member of clubs and organizations (Manning, 1989). Such exclusionary practices are chilling reminders of deeply entrenched, institutionalized beliefs about the worth and status of individuals because of their gender, race, ethnicity, or sexual orientation.

Annual events (e.g., award ceremonies) may contain messages celebrating adherence to norms defined by a singular, dominant cultural perspective (Katz, 1989; Schaef, 1985). A college's espoused commitment to celebrate diversity (Garland, 1985; Hodgkinson, 1985; Smith, 1989) entreats administrators, students, graduates, and faculty to examine traditions to insure that these events acknowledge the culturally unique accomplishments of, for example, gay men and lesbians, women, students of color and other historically underrepresented groups (Kuh, et al., 1991).

Cultural artifacts carry many messages that conflict with espoused values. An example of negative messages embodied in a ritual can be found in Kake Walk, a University of Vermont tradition that began in 1893 until it was terminated in 1969. Yet, the memory of Kake Walk persists. Kake Walk, including the performers' black-face make-up, was a parody of late nineteenth-century minstrel shows. Primarily a fraternity and sorority event, "kake walkers" would practice their high-stepping routines for months in preparation for the event which routinely attracted 5,000 students, administrators, graduates, and local citizens. The racist message of Kake Walk, clearly evident in the re-enactment of slaves' perfor- mances to win the cake provided by their masters, was *not* viewed as being racist in intent by many attending the annual event. "To be sure, no participant thought Kake Walk was racist. Defenders argued that since the walkers didn't *intend* to be racist, they could not be racist" (Loewen, 1990, p. 15).

There is a lesson to be learned from the ongoing lamentations by graduates and Vermont natives about the demise of Kake Walk. Over its 76 year existence, the event was one of the few activities which brought together various groups from the institution, city, and state in ways that nothing else did. Because Kake Walk was declared to be "not intentionally racist," it was not easy to elimi- nate; its racist messages were confounded with positive messages of community, loyalty, unity, and entertainment. But in 1969, the student newspaper declared: 'No amount of tradition and longevity can be used as a defense for the continuation of Kake Walk.' They knew that if Kake Walk had ever been a unifying activity, it could unify no longer (Loewen, 1990, p. 14-15).

That Kake Walk was deeply rooted at the University of Vermont is a lesson that even long-standing, valued traditions that send *positive* messages can no longer be tolerated *if* unacceptable mes- sages are *simultaneously* conveyed. Campus traditions that seem to promote unity but also tacitly endorse racism, sexism, and homophobia warrant critical evaluation.

PERSPECTIVES

The previous section described cultural artifacts, the more tan- gible manifestations of campus culture. This section provides ex- amples of perspectives, the "shared rules and norms applicable to a given context," including the "social conventions manifested through behavior" (Chapter 1). It is at the perspective level (e.g., unwritten rules, norms) that behavior endorsed by the student cul- ture often clashes with the values of faculty and administrative cultures. Examples of perspectives include expectations for student, administrative, and faculty behavior and principles upon which community members order their activities.

Horowitz (1987) and Moffatt (1989) described campus culture from the students' point of view. Using student perspectives as a frame of reference, Horowitz argued that the "college man" sub-culture originated in the 19th century and embraced persistent themes of American youth culture, such as accepting attitudes toward alcohol and drug use, the college years as a time for experimentation, and a grade orientation coupled with disinterest in intellectual matters. In short, the college man culture, which continues to dominate many residential campuses, is interested primarily in the social aspects of college life and disdainful of academic pursuits.

Based on her analysis of "college man" culture, it is not surprising that Horowitz (1984) was critical of fraternities; they perpetuate behavior antithetical to the academic ethos (e.g., excessive drinking, hazing, pledging). Student affairs professionals have long wrestled with the myth of indestructibility that permeates youth and student cultures and encourages students to ignore the potential consequences of dangerous activities (e.g., alcoholism, death or injury, sexually transmitted disease). Administrators and faculty have attempted, with varying degrees of success, to change these hedonistic, deep-seated attitudes, particularly those about alcohol, multiculturalism, and sometimes violent behavior. The perspective of youth toward life as immortal is difficult to assail.

However, cultural properties can be used to counter "college man" messages, including expectations about inclusion and multiculturalism, self-control, responsible use of alcohol, and enhanced expectations for academic achievement. On some campuses, peer mobilization has been successful in modifying aspects of the "college man" culture. For example, student groups such as SADD (Students Against Drunk Driving) have had a constructive influence on reducing hazardous use of alcohol. Interventions that in the past have been dismissed as boring and ineffective (e.g., non-alcoholic pubs, alternative mixers, comedy clubs) seem to be working and, as a result, are becoming more popular initiatives to change the student culture. These positive counter-images offer alternative conceptions of heroes and heroines to be celebrated, constructive reflections of campus life, and productive portrayals of institutional values upon which the students can model their behavior. We shall return to these themes in Chapter 6 and 7.

VALUES

Values are the "espoused as well as the enacted ideals of an institution or group and serve as the basis on which members of a culture or subculture judge situations, acts, objects, and people" (Chapter 1). Community, commitment to the environment, women's leadership, and religious values of a church-related college are examples of cultural values. In the following paragraphs, community, a value vigorously endorsed by most institutions, is used to illustrate the importance of campus culture.

Whether intentional or unintentional, people bond to one another and to the institution through participation in such cultural performances as telling stories about their college and its heroes and heroines. Events such as homecoming, May Day at Earlham College, and Picnic Day at University of California, Davis (Mechling & Wilson, 1988) not only communicate the importance attached to the concept of community, but also nurture and sustain community (Kuh et al., 1991). "Community must not only be created but recreated continually in institutions of higher education, and ritual has a vital role to play" (Carnegie Foundation for the Advancement of Teaching, 1990, p. 55). The need to connect with the college is very important for many students as it is this sense of belonging— of feeling like one is a full member of the institution—that contributes to self-esteem, establishes a context in which relationships are formed, and nurtures emotional attachments among students and with the institution.

How the values of groups differ can be seen by comparing faculty culture with student affairs culture. The core values of collegial decision making, peer evaluation, and academic freedom are deeply rooted in academic life and influence how faculty perform their teaching, research, and service functions. Although a debate continues about the relative importance of the contributions of student affairs to the purposes of higher education (Manning, in press), the core values of academics and student affairs professionals seem to have become more compatible over the past 15 years. In part, this rapprochement is a result of concerted efforts by faculty and administrators who serve as boundary spanners between the two cultures, translating and explaining the activities of each group to the other. Some of the differences in values that persist between faculty and student affairs can be attributed, in part, to differences about what constitutes a quality education and the relative worth of experiences outside of the classroom. Cultural differences of faculty and student affairs will be addressed in more depth in Chapter 4.

ASSUMPTIONS

The most basic level of culture exists in the assumptions and beliefs upon which an institution's policies and practices are based. Assumptions include beliefs about equity in the treatment of students and colleagues, accepted modes of behaving, and presumptions about fairness among institutional members. A topic of discussion on many college campuses is whether the cultural assumptions upon which the majority of colleges are organized are consistent with a commitment to multiculturalism (Altbach & Lomotey, 1991; Bennett, 1984; Berman, 1992; Bloom, 1987; Steele, 1990).

The earliest American colleges and universities were established using assumptions based on a European model to prepare men to be ministers and teachers (Fenske, 1989). With such notable exceptions as historically Black and women's institutions, institutions founded in the 17th and 18th centuries were characterized typically by Christian beliefs, hierarchical and paternalistic organizational systems, and a Euro-American centered curriculum. These underlying assumptions fuel cultural messages or "tacit beliefs that members use to define their role, their relationships to others, and the nature of the organization" (Chapter 1). Although colleges and universities serve different purposes today, the roots of masculine heritage run deep and are evident in many of traditions of the fraternity system as well as the overrepresentation of men in senior administrative positions.

Some of these assumptions, manifested in cultural artifacts, are no longer congruent with student characteristics and the missions of most institutions. For example, Princeton University's Eating Clubs, established when the University was single-sex, remain open only to men. The assumptions upon which these clubs are based are inconsistent with Princeton's present co-educational student body. Although admissions practices reflect an educational philosophy that embraces coeducation, the university's ethos remains heavily influenced by the institution's male heritage.

As students and faculty become more diverse, student affairs professionals must become more adept at identifying and responding to those cultural assumptions that are antithetical to their institution's mission and aspirations. Skill in determining cultural assumptions also is essential for meeting the needs of diverse students. For students of diverse backgrounds (e.g., women, African

Americans, rural students, adult students, commuters), a college's culture may be at odds with their own backgrounds and past experiences; such conflicts can be oppressive and isolating. The ethos of a particular college, given the shifting demographics in American higher education, must be examined in light of assumptions about equity, community, and goals for student learning and personal development.

IMPLICATIONS FOR STUDENT AFFAIRS PROFESSIONALS

Student affairs administrators are well positioned to address the following questions. How is the college's mission and philosophy expressed through cultural practices? Do students, staff, and faculty know the institution's mission, not through reading the college catalog but from awareness of its expression in everyday practice? Are cultural messages confused and contradictory? Can all members of the institution explain what the college stands for? What is the image of a graduate of my institution? What images of the "college man" continue to be impressed upon parents and new students? What are the assumptions that underlie administrative practice? What are the assumptions that underlie academic practice?

The answers to the above questions, discovered through a reflexive examination of administrative and academic goals and actions, channel administrative- and student-based actions which perpetuate the campus culture. An examination of the clarity and expressiveness of a college's assumptions can reveal its capabilities in carrying out its stated mission.

Cultural activities bind people in a celebration of founding ideals, commitment, and community. Emotions evoked during an event become memories not only of that event but later are generalized to feelings about the institution. As a result, students, faculty, and administrators link themselves to purposes larger than themselves by creating an emotional bond between and among the different groups of participants and the institution. In this way, students, faculty members, and administrators become wed to the ideals and values of the institution (Manning, 1989).

Knowledge of cultural artifacts, the messages conveyed, and the institution's underlying assumptions can be used by student affairs professionals to foster student learning and personal development. The task of choosing images, metaphors, and language that appropriately represent institutional values and purposes is challenging. "There are no rules for such representation, for the explication and interpretation of reality" (Greenfield, 1984, p. 156). Student affairs professionals must increase their understanding of cultures as well as how cultural artifacts shape student thought and action. Rather than assuming that the messages of traditional events and practices are positive for all students, cultural analysis of the assumptions undergirding these events must be undertaken. Thus, an emerging role for student affairs administrators is to critically examine whether the messages conveyed by their campus culture are consistent with desired college values and beliefs. This point will be addressed in Chapter 7.

Activities

In an effort to identify and learn about different aspects of campus culture, the reader is encouraged to participate in some or all of the following activities:

1. Take part in a cultural immersion exercise; that is, spend time in a culture other than your own. Depending on your ethnicity, sexual orientation, or physical character, activities might include spending the day blindfolded, attending meetings of a gay and lesbian organization, or attending services at an African American church.

2. Take a walking tour of campus and try to put into words the "sense of place" you experience. Be sure to describe what you feel rather than just what you see.

3. Observe commencement from a parent's perspective. What does the college stand for? What are the values that are expressed? Are the messages inclusionary or exclusionary? How is language used?

4. Inventory the most powerful cultural activities on your campus with an eye toward who participates in various events. Who is missing? What are the values being communicated that might explain the absence of members from certain groups?

5. Conduct informal research about how traditional events are supported and perpetuated by the administration. Do these events complement the mission and purposes of the institution? How do the events sustain the campus culture?

6. Conduct informal research about how traditional events are supported and perpetuated by students. Ask questions similar to number five above but from a student perspective.

References

Altbach, P., & Lomotey, K. (1991). *The racial crisis in American higher education.* Albany, NY: The State University of New York Press.

Babcock, B. (1984). Arrange me into disorder: Fragments and reflections of ritual clowning. In J. MacAloon (Ed.), *Rite, drama, festival, spectacle: Rehearsals toward a theory of cultural performances* (pp. 102–128). Philadelphia, PA: Institution for the Study of Human Issues.

Bennett, W. (1984). *To reclaim a legacy.* Washington, D.C.: National Endowment for the Arts.

Berman, P. (1992). *Debating P.C..* New York, NY: Dell.

Bloom, A. (1987). *Closing of the American mind.* New York, NY: Simon and Schuster.

Carnegie Foundation for the Advancement of Teaching. (1990). *Campus life: In search of community.* Princeton, NJ: Author.

Clark, B. (1963). Faculty organization and authority. In T. Lumsford (Ed.) *The study of academic administration* (pp. 37–51). Western Interstate Commission for Higher Education.

Clark, B. (1972). The organizational saga in higher education. *Administrative Science Quarterly, 17*(2), 178–184.

Fenske, R. (1989). Historical foundations of student services. In G. Hanson and U. Delworth (Eds.), *Student services: A handbook for the profession* (pp. 5–24). San Francisco, CA: Jossey-Bass.

Fernandez, J. (1988). Andalusia on our minds: Two contrasting places in Spain as seen in a vernacular poetic duel of the late 19th century. *Cultural Anthropology, 3*(1), 21–35.

Garland, P. (1985). *Serving more than students: A critical need for student personnel services.* ASHE-ERIC Higher Education Report, No. 7. Washington, D.C.: Association for the Study of Higher Education.

Greenfield, T. (1984). Leaders and schools: Willfulness and nonnatural order in organizations. In T. Sergiovanni, and J. Corbally, (Eds.), *Leadership and organizational cultures: New perspectives on administrative theory and practice.* (pp. 125–141). Urbana, IL: University of Illinois Press.

Hodgkinson, H. (1985). *All one system: Demographics of education, kindergarten through graduate school.* Washington, D.C.: The Institute for Educational Leadership, Inc.

Horowitz, H.L. (1984). *Alma mater: Design and experience in the women's colleges from their nineteenth–century beginnings to the 1930s.* New York, NY: Knopf.

Horowitz, H.L. (1987). *Campus life: Undergraduate cultures from the end of the eighteenth century to the present.* Chicago, IL: University of Chicago Press.

Kapferer, B. (1984). The ritual process and the problem of reflexivity in Sinhalese demon exorcisms. In J. MacAloon (Ed.), *Rite, drama, festival, spectacle: Rehearsals toward a theory of cultural performance* (pp. 179–207). Philadelphia, PA: Institution for the Study of Human Issues.

Katz, J.H. (1989). The challenge of diversity. In C. Woolbright (Ed.). *Valuing diversity* (pp. 1-21). Bloomington, IN: Association of College Unions-International.

Kuh, G. D., Schuh, J. H., Whitt, E. J. & Associates (1991). *Involving colleges: Successful approaches for fostering student learning and development outside the classroom.* San Francisco: Jossey-Bass.

Kuh, G. D., & Whitt, E. J. (1988). *The invisible tapestry: Culture in American colleges and universities.* ASHE-ERIC Higher Education Report, No. 1. Washington, D.C.: Association for the Study of Higher Education.

Lewis, A. (1980). The ritual process and community development. *Community Development Journal, 15*(3), 190–199.

Loewen, J. (1990). "A-walkin' fo' de kake": The history of Kake Walk. *Vermont Sunday Magazine*, p. 4.

MacAloon, B. (Ed.), (1984). *Rite, drama, festival, spectacle: Rehearsals toward a theory of cultural performance.* Philadelphia, PA: Institution for the Study of Human Issues.

Maisel, J.M. (1990). Social fraternities and sororities are not conducive to the educational process. *NASPA Journal, 28*(1), 8–12.

Manning, K. (1989). *Campus rituals and cultural meaning.* Unpublished doctoral dissertation. Bloomington, IN: Indiana University.

Manning, K. (in press). Rethinking the introduction to student affairs course. *NASPA Journal.*

Mechling, J., & Wilson, D. S. (1988). Organizational festivals and the uses of ambiguity: The case of Picnic Day at Davis. In M. Jones, M. Moore and R. Snyder (Eds.), *Inside organizations: Understanding the human dimension* (pp. 303–317). Newbury Park, CA: Sage.

Moffatt, M. (1989). *Coming of age in New Jersey.* New Brunswick, NJ: Rutgers University Press.

Schaef, A.W. (1985). *Women's reality.* Minneapolis, MN: Winston.

Smith, D. (1989). *The challenge of diversity: Involvement or alienation in the academy?* ASHE-ERIC Higher Education Report, No. 5. Washington, D.C.: School of Education and Human Development, The George Washington University.

Steele, S. (1990). *The content of our character.* New York, NY: St. Martin's Press.

Thelin, J. R., & Yankovich, J. (1987). Bricks and mortar: Architecture and the study of higher education. In J. Smart (Ed.), *Higher education: Handbook of theory and research,* Vol. III (pp. 57–83). New York: Agathon.

van Gennep, A. (1960). *The rites of passage.* Chicago, IL: University of Chicago Press.

CHAPTER 3

Side by Side: Faculty and Student Affairs Cultures

Patrick G. Love
George D. Kuh
Kathleen A. MacKay
Christine M. Hardy

On many campuses the divisions of student affairs and academic affairs operate independently. At some institutions, these administrative units virtually ignore each other. This separation often is characterized by infrequent contact between faculty and student affairs professionals, a lack of knowledge and disinterest on the part of faculty about the purposes and functions of student affairs, and frustration expressed by both faculty and student affairs professionals about what appear to be skewed priorities in the distribution of institutional resources. Although these two groups work at the same institution with the same students, they sometimes act as if they are in different worlds.

Consider these situations:

> One Monday afternoon you [a student affairs professional] receive a call from Dr. Smith, a physics professor at your institution who you know well. "[Your name], something has come up and I have to go out of town. I was wondering if you could teach my introductory physics class for me tomorrow morning?" What would you be feeling at that moment? Astonishment? Fear? Anxiety? Dread? Those are the same feelings that many faculty feel when a student affairs staff members asks: "Professor, would you like to have dinner tonight with the students in the dining hall?" (Overheard at a national student affairs conference)

Going to the dining hall was a horrible experience for me. The staff member told me to grab a tray and food and just sit with some students. I had no idea how to get through the line and felt foolish. Then when I stood in the middle of the room looking for a seat, I felt like I was in a restaurant and was expected to invite myself to join people in their meal. I felt more out of place than the first time I visited Ahmadabad, India. I never went back [to the dining hall]. (professor of anthropology, liberal arts college in the northeast)

These stories suggest at least one false assumption on the part of student affairs professionals—that faculty are comfortable in student dining halls. This lack of understanding can be attributed, in part, to the differences between the cultures of faculty and student affairs. For student affairs professionals to successfully build bridges between the in-class and out-of-class experiences of students, they must first understand and appreciate faculty and student affairs cultures.

The purpose of this chapter is to examine selected aspects of faculty and student affairs cultures. Similarities and differences in the cultures of faculty and student affairs will be highlighted including observations about why collaboration between members of these two groups often has been difficult to achieve. Finally, suggestions are made about how to use cultural perspectives to enhance mutual understanding and collaboration between student affairs professionals and faculty.

FACULTY CULTURE

Multiple layers of faculty culture exist. In this section three faculty cultures will be delineated: (a) the culture of the academic profession; (b) the culture of the institution and of institutional type; and (c) the culture of the discipline (Austin, 1990). Other influences on faculty culture (e.g., gender, type of appointment) also will be briefly considered.

The Culture of the Academic Profession

Considerable variance exists in the personal values and beliefs of faculty (Bowen & Schuster, 1986). For example, Ladd and Lipset (1975) found that social scientists tended to be fairly liberal in their thinking compared with faculty from professional fields who were likely to be somewhat conservative. Even so, most scholars agree that faculty share certain values and beliefs that characterize the essence of what it means to be an academic (Austin, 1990; Becher, 1987). Although there has been some debate about whether an overall faculty culture exists across institutional type and disciplines (cf. Light, 1974), three primary faculty values have been identified: (a) the pursuit and dissemination of knowledge as the primary goal of higher education; (b) professional autonomy including the importance of academic freedom; and (c) collegiality expressed through self-governance (Austin, 1990; Becher, 1987; Bowen & Schuster, 1986; Clark, 1963; Kuh & Whitt, 1988).

Academics seek and disseminate knowledge through a variety of means; most efforts can be classified according to one or more of the activities in the classic triad of faculty work—teaching, research, and service. What constitutes knowledge and the appropriate ways to disseminate knowledge vary by discipline Becher, 1987). As we shall see shortly, faculty at various types of institutions have different priorities for teaching and research. Nonetheless, the value of generating and sharing knowledge is central to all faculty.

Another cornerstone of faculty culture is professional autonomy. "For the most part, faculty view themselves as individualists. They are solitary, even reclusive, in their work. Each faculty member has their own thing to do and would prefer to be left alone to do it" (Mills, 1987, p. 9). Baldridge, Curtis, Ecker and Riley (1978) emphasized that faculty expect to have autonomy; the greater the faculty member's expertise the greater one's professional autonomy. The value of autonomy is expressed by the faculty's commitment to perpetuating of the peer review process and tenure system (Whitt, 1988). A flexible work schedule and independent research or writing time are additional indicators of autonomy.

The third faculty value, collegiality, is commonly demonstrated through commitment to faculty governance. Faculty view their institution as a community of scholars which provides faculty with support and opportunities for social and intellectual interaction. However, fewer faculty seem to be participating actively in faculty governance compared with past cohorts of academics (Bowen & Schuster, 1986). Nevertheless, attempts to increase administrative controls on faculty activity or to eliminate tenure almost always prompts collective action by faculty members.

According to Austin and Gamson (1983), intrinsic factors such as autonomy and academic freedom are more important to faculty members than extrinsic factors, such as workload or reward structure. And although these values—pursuit and dissemination of knowledge, autonomy, and collegiality—vary in strength from campus to campus, they work together to form the core of a faculty member's professional identity.

Institutionally-based Faculty Cultures

The type, size, and history of a college or university provides another perspective on faculty culture. Faculty tend to gravitate to the size and type of institution that complements their own values and beliefs. For example, "institutions with salient missions [such] as teaching colleges. . . attract faculty who are willing to invest themselves in those students and missions" (Kuh et al., 1991, p. 175).

Through promotion and reward processes, research institutions emphasize scholarly productivity over teaching as the primary method of disseminating knowledge. Boyer (1987) found that more than one quarter of the faculty at research universities do not teach undergraduate courses. Bowen and Schuster (1986) used the practice of using money from grants to "buy" release time from teaching as additional evidence of the valuing of research over teaching at research universities. Although the institutional missions at small liberal arts colleges usually emphasize teaching and the education of the whole person (Kuh & Whitt, 1988), even at these institutions, research and publication are more highly valued and rewarded than teaching (Boyer, 1987). Faculty at community colleges have the clearest sense of purpose and agreement regarding academic values (Boyer, 1987); they believe that teaching is more important than research and that teaching effectiveness should be the primary criterion for promotion.

As with student culture (Chapter 4), the faculty culture at a given institution is rarely monolithic. Larger and more complex institutions are more likely than smaller colleges to have multiple faculty subcultures rather than a single, unified faculty culture (Clark, 1963). These subcultures may be based on discipline (described later), gender, length of service (e.g., tenured vs. non-tenured faculty), type of appointment (e.g., part-time faculty), or commitment to collective bargaining and unionization (Ruscio, 1987). Some of these faculty subcultures are discussed below.

Discipline-based Faculty Cultures

In the late 19th century, institutional missions became more diverse and the number of courses, departments, and disciplines proliferated (Metzger, 1987). Science begot chemistry, biology, and geology. Biology begot botany, genetics, and anatomy. Disciplines became differentiated in the content of their subject matters and accepted modes of argument and research (Becher, 1987). Because faculty members learn what it means to be an academic as they are socialized to their discipline, it is not surprising that many faculty began to identify more closely with their discipline than with their institution (Clark, 1963). "The culture of the discipline is the primary source of faculty identity and expertise and typically engenders stronger bonds than those developed with the institution of employment, particularly in large universities" (Kuh & Whitt, 1988, p. 77). Faculty subcultures (Dill, 1982) also were nurtured by the development of national academic associations organized by discipline, such as the Modern Language Association and the American Psychological Association (Metzger, 1987). As a result, the hegemony that characterized faculty attitudes and role orientation in the early 20th century began to dissolve as faculty were serving two masters, their institution and their discipline.

Before one can become a contributing member of disciplinary culture, the discipline's language and practices must be mastered, something which usually occurs during graduate school and the first faculty position (Bess, 1982; Clark, 1984; Freedman, 1979). Artifacts of discipline-based faculty culture include specialized language, intellectual traditions and style, and discipline-specific folklore (Becher, 1987).

The narrowing of subject matter required more specialized training (Blau, 1973; Clark, 1984; Morrill & Spees, 1982) which resulted in increased isolation of faculty (Dill, 1982) and decreased communication across disciplines. Unlike other professions (e.g., doctors, lawyers), where entry into the profession starts with common training of all those entering and then proceeds to specialization, an academic career begins with specialization through the choice of department and subject at the outset of graduate training. This early graduate specialization contributes to the isolation of one subject area from another. As faculty members focus more on their specific scholarly interests, they are less likely to know and appreciate subjects other than their own. Without constant and meaningful communication, it is difficult for the professorate to maintain a unified set of assumptions and beliefs (Dill, 1982). Thus, it should not be surprising that some student affairs practitioners have difficulty communicating with faculty when faculty across disciplines are experiencing difficulty communicating with each other.

Other Influences on Faculty Culture

Two additional aspects of the academic profession that influence faculty cultures merit attention: the nature of the faculty appointment and gender.

Part-time and adjunct faculty. A part-time faculty member is defined as someone who teaches less than a full course load. An adjunct faculty member can be either full- or part-time and is typically hired on a year-to-year basis but is not eligible for tenure. For the purposes of this section, the term adjunct faculty includes both part-time and adjunct faculty.

Adjunct faculty are the gypsies of the academic profession, teaching on a fill-in, as-needed basis. They may be recent graduates seeking experience to make them more attractive for a tenure-track position; they may be local professionals with experience, but lacking the credentials of full-time faculty; or they may be retired faculty wishing to remain connected to the institution and/or their discipline. Typically, adjuncts are not expected to engage in research and service activities.

Adjunct faculty have existed in higher education for a long time. Until relatively recently their numbers at most institutions were small and they had little influence on the overall faculty culture. However, changes in student demographics and financial conditions have contributed to an increase in the use of adjunct faculty (Boyer, 1987). Given their tenuous relationship to the institution and lack of status and financial benefits they seldom develop a sense of loyalty to the institution or its clientele (Boyer, 1987). When the number of adjunct faculty at an institution is high, the faculty voice becomes less coherent and the sense of community and shared educational purpose diminishes. Whether adjunct faculty at a particular institution qualify as a subculture (see Chapter 4) is questionable; they do not often interact with each other or with regular faculty, do not participate in institutional governance, and are, therefore, unconnected to the institution.

Female faculty culture. There is growing evidence that female faculty members are developing a culture that cuts across institutional and disciplinary boundaries. Beliefs and assumptions shared by female faculty include being an outsider to the dominant faculty culture, highly valuing the "soft" subjects (e.g., history, anthropology, education), appreciating various methodological approaches, and assuming personal responsibility for balancing personal life and professional commitments (Aisenberg & Harrington, 1988; Chamberlain, 1988; Pearson, Shavlik, & Touchton, 1988). Associating these beliefs and values with female faculty is not to say that some male faculty members do not hold similar values and beliefs, rather that they appear to be of greater significance to a majority of female faculty.

Although women have participated in higher education for many decades, they have not been viewed as equal partners. The majority of women faculty are non-tenured assistant professors (Chamberlain, 1988); the number of women presently in tenured full professor positions is low (Pearson, Shavlik, & Touchton, 1988), so women have a limited number of female role models. As a result, the majority of female faculty members are outside the power structure of the academy, many feel as though they are "informed outsiders" (Aisenberg & Harrington, 1988, p. 86).

Women academics are concentrated in what are commonly called "traditionally female fields" (Chamberlain, 1988), including education, social work, library science, and nursing. These service-oriented fields examine the human experience and are not highly valued in the academic hierarchy (Chamberlain, 1988). Yet female faculty, in significantly greater percentages than men, continue to seek training in the "soft" subjects despite the low status of these fields. This commitment also carries with it a willingness to utilize various methodological approaches in research (Aisenberg & Harrington, 1988) including qualitative methods which are based on premises inconsistent with the linear scientific (and male dominated) thinking which continues to be valued in most colleges and universities.

More so than men, perhaps, female faculty members invest considerable energy trying to balance their personal and professional commitments. Sociologists who have studied working women and the division of personal and family responsibilities such as childcare and household duties found that women are responsible for the majority of the workload (Gerson, 1985; Hochschild, 1989); this also holds for female faculty (Chamberlain, 1988). With women assuming the majority of family and home responsibilities, they often use time for non-faculty tasks that could be devoted to research or teaching.

The culture of academe remains dominated by traditionally masculine values. As the number of female faculty members increases it is possible that those traditional masculine values may be modified or that, in addition to fragmenting along disciplinary lines, the faculty culture may continue to fragment along gender lines.

Summary

"By its nature, the culture of any group of human beings is complicated, fluid, and endlessly resistant to scientific descriptions. . . [S]cholars who want to understand cultural settings must be willing to accept uncertainty and ambiguity" (Aisenberg & Harrington, 1988, p. 92). To understand the faculty culture at a particular institution one must consider the type of institution, the institution's history and traditions, influences beyond the institution (e.g., the culture of the discipline), and other factors (e.g., the role of part time faculty, and the number and influence of female faculty). Differences in socialization experiences, values, and assumptions may result in faculty viewing their role, the institution, and students in ways that differ from student affairs professionals. Failure to recognize and appreciate the cultural differences between various groups of faculty will make communicating with faculty members unnecessarily difficult and frustrating, and successful collaboration much less likely. By the same token, student affairs professionals must understand their own cultures, the topic to which we now turn.

STUDENT AFFAIRS CULTURE

The roots of the student affairs profession date back more than a century to the appointment of the first Dean of Men at Harvard in 1870. Since that time the roles and tasks of student affairs practitioners have proliferated and diversified. In this section the characterstics of student affairs cultures are discussed. Variations in cultural properties by functional area and institutional type also are addressed.

Culture of the Student Affairs Profession

Unlike the faculty culture, there is no generally accepted set of core values for student affairs. In fact, identifying the guiding beliefs and assumptions for the student affairs profession has generated a considerable discussion and debate (Kuh, Shedd, & Whitt, 1987; Stamatakos, 1981a, 1981b; Stamatakos & Rogers, 1984). Winston and Saunders (1991) took an extreme view:

> With few exceptions, the student affairs profession has not been introspective, nor analytical, concerning its philosophy and values. Generally speaking, student affairs professionals have been "doers," not "thinkers." As a consequence no first-rate philosophical analysis of the field's assumptions, beliefs, and values has yet appeared (p. 319).

Winston and Saunders (1991) suggested that three documents provide basic statements of values and philosophy: *The Student Personnel Point of View, The Student Personnel Point of View, Revised Edition*, and "Student Development Services in Post Secondary Education." Winston and Saunders (1991) also identified four diverse philosophical traditions within the student affairs literature: holism (the student is a whole person), humanism (belief in human rationality, the possibility of human perfection, and the value of self-awareness and self-understanding), pragmatism (making things work), and individualism (recognition of and appreciation for individual differences in backgrounds, abilities, interests, and goals).

A committee appointed in 1986 by the National Association of Student Personnel Administrators (NASPA) identified the following core assumptions of the student affairs profession:

- Each student is unique;
- Each person has worth and dignity;
- Bigotry cannot be tolerated;
- Feelings affect thinking and learning;
- Student involvement enhances learning;
- Personal circumstances affect learning;
- Out-of-class environments affect learning;
- A supportive and friendly community life helps students learn;
- The freedom to doubt and question must be protected;

- Effective citizenship should be taught; and
- Students are responsible for their own lives (NASPA, 1987, pp. 9-13).

It can be argued that these assumptions are ideals to which the profession aspires and, therefore, reflect espoused values rather than guiding assumptions that are enacted in daily actions.

Kitchner (1985) presented a set of ethical principles for student affairs practitioners that reflect some of the values of the profession: (1) respect autonomy; (2) do no harm; (3) benefit others; (4) be just (i.e., assure equal treatment for those in our charge); and (5) be faithful (i.e., keep promises, tell the truth, be loyal, maintain respect and civility in human discourse). Finally, Eickmann (1988) offered yet another set of espoused values for student affairs: commitment to excellence; commitment to learning and growth; commitment to integrity (personal, intellectual, institutional); and commitment to high quality.

Although consensus may not exist concerning the enacted values and basic assumptions of the student affairs profession, some common threads emerge. These include a commitment to the development of the whole student including basic and developmental needs, active learning and participation, and the importance of accepting and celebrating human differences.

Institution-based Student Affairs Culture

As with faculty, the type of institution and its history and traditions influence the culture of a student affairs division. Community colleges serve a highly diverse student body; most commute and many are older, married, or work full-time. As a result, the nature of programs and support services required to address the various needs of students may be quite different than at other types of institutions.

Professionals at small liberal arts colleges are likely to be generalists, responsible for more than one area of student affairs or a greater portion of the department in which they work (e.g., the director of residence life who also makes housing assignments and is responsible for building maintenance) (Goffigon, Lacey, Wright & Kuh, 1986). When student affairs professionals have frequent contact with students, the student affairs division is more likely to be perceived as nurturing and caring. A tradition of attention can become one of the many threads woven into the tapestry of an institution's culture (McAleenan & Kuh, 1986). Also, the institutional missions of small colleges are often distinctive, and convey institutional values which student affairs staff are expected to endorse personally and professionally.

Most large institutions have a sizable number of staff with professional preparation. Because student affairs functions in such institutions tend to be specialized, student affairs professionals usually deal with more narrow aspects of the student's experience (e.g., judicial affairs, orientation, or alcohol and drug education). Such specialization makes it difficult for a staff member to view students holistically and to spend quality time with individual students. In addition, the various student services provided on a large campus are more likely to be located in different buildings. When student affairs functions are physically separated, there are fewer opportunities for student affairs professionals to interact with each other on a face-to-face basis; thus, it is more difficult for staff to develop a common language and a coherent set of common values, beliefs, and assumptions.

Functional Areas

Just as academic disciplines proliferated in higher education during the last century, there is evidence that specialties are multiplying within student affairs. As with the relationship between faculty, disciplines, and institutions, it is likely that some student affairs professionals forge closer links with their specialization than student affairs as a field of professional practice or their institution. For example, financial aid administrators may have more in common (and, therefore, stronger cultural ties) with financial aid administrators on other campuses than with student affairs colleagues on their own campus.

Love (1990) explored the culture of a residence life department at a midwestern urban university. Among the values shared by the residence life staff there were student service, willingness to innovate, accessibility to students, and autonomy. He also identified a student affairs values continuum. Individuals who valued the developmental and programmatic aspects of their work were clustered at one end of the continuum; at the other end were individuals who valued the administrative and facilities aspects of their job. Most student affairs professionals cluster on the developmental and programmatic end of the continuum (e.g., student activities, orienta-

tion, Greek-letter affairs, counseling, career planning and placement). It is risky to make definitive statements about the cultural
properties of student affairs functional areas in the absence of research. However, recognizing the likelihood that values, beliefs,
and assumptions vary from department to department is an important step toward becoming sensitive to different aspects of the student affairs cultures on a given campus.

Educational Preparation and Involvement in Professional Associations

Professionals are socialized in many ways, such as through paraprofessional experiences (e.g., resident advisor), professional preparation programs, full-time professional employment at one or more
institutions, and professional organizations. Therefore, additional
factors that affect the student affairs culture on a given campus are
the preparation of staff and the involvement of student affairs staff
in professional organizations.

One consideration is the balance of professionals with bachelor's
degrees, and those with advanced degrees from student affairs preparation programs, or in related fields (e.g., counseling, social work),
or in unrelated fields. Professionals bring to their jobs the values,
beliefs, and assumptions of their "cultures of orientation" (Van
Maanen, 1984)—their fields of professional preparation—whether
student affairs or some other area. That some student affairs staff
have training in disciplines other than student affairs and higher
education is not necessarily problematic. New and different experiences and challenges invigorate the student affairs field (Kuh &
Schuh, 1991; Kuh, Whitt, & Shedd, 1987). However, divergent
values, beliefs, and assumptions can have a fragmenting influence
on the student affairs culture at a given institution. For example,
an individual with an MBA may have very different assumptions
and values than someone with a counseling-based student affairs
master's degree and, therefore, these two people may find it difficult to work closely together unless they discuss and understand
these basic differences.

Professional organizations also shape the values, beliefs, and
assumptions of the student affairs culture on a given campus. For
example, aspects of the national student affairs culture are reflected
in conference themes, keynote addresses, program offerings, and
journals and other publications. Professional associations also in-

troduce new ideas and technologies to an institution as staff take part in regional and national meetings and transport these ideas to their campus upon their return. As a result, the philosophy and role orientation of staff who are involved in professional associations may differ from the philosophy and role orientation of staff who are not active in association work beyond the campus. The former are similar to Gouldner's (1957) "cosmopolitan" faculty (identify with the discipline and colleagues on a national level); the latter are more like "locals" whose primary allegiance is to the institution.

Numerous associations with a specialized focus have formed in the last several decades (e.g., National Orientation Directors Association, Association for Student Judicial Affairs). The number of standing committees and commissions within ACPA and NASPA continues to grow. As these specialty groups mature, they may develop traditions, values, beliefs, and assumptions that differentiate them from other groups, and, in some cases, from the larger profession. Indeed, some have speculated that there are cultural differences between some organizations (e.g., NASPA is oriented to institutional needs, ACPA is oriented to needs of entry-level staff and students). However, without definitive cultural research on these groups, it is premature to draw conclusions.

Information about the academic and experiential preparation of staff members (e.g., master's in student affairs versus a bachelor's in accounting for a financial aid counselor), or the professional organizations with which staff identify, provides clues to the values of various offices in the student affairs division. If, for example, counseling center staff members identify with the American Association of Counseling and Development or the American Psychological Association, rather than with the American College Personnel Association, their basic values, beliefs, behaviors, and assumptions may differ from those of other student affairs practitioners; in part these differences may be due to the values, beliefs, assumptions, and expectations promoted by the different professional organizations.

Summary

To date, relatively little attention has been given to identifying the cultural elements of the student affairs profession. Documents

addressing the philosophy, values, and assumptions of student affairs provide a frame of reference with which staff can examine
and interpret their campus culture. Recognizing that cultural differences exist among the various types of institutions, departments,
and professional associations is a key step in the continuing exploration of cultural influences on professional practice.

INTERACTION BETWEEN FACULTY AND STUDENT AFFAIRS CULTURE

In this section the basic values underlying the cultures of faculty and of student affairs are compared to better understand the
two cultures (see also Kuh, Shedd & Whitt, 1987). Consideration
is given to how the two groups view each other and themselves
and how, through use of cultural perspectives, student affairs professionals can improve their communication and collaboration with
faculty colleagues.

Comparison of Values

The following table suggests that the basic values of faculty and
student affairs differ in some important ways.

Prime Faculty Values	Prime Student Affairs Values
1. Creation and dissemination of knowledge (teaching and research, focus on higher order needs)	Holistic student development (active learning, programming, challenge and support, focus on both basic and higher order needs)
2. Autonomy over collaboration	Collaboration over autonomy
3. Collegiality (self-governance, flat hierarchy)	Teamwork (acceptance of structure and differentiated hierarchy)
4. Thinking and reflecting over doing	Doing over thinking and reflecting

The two groups clearly differ on the first value. Faculty members value and focus their energies on higher order needs of their
students. Student affairs professionals focus on both basic needs

(e.g., orienting students to the institution, providing them with places to live and eat, helping them obtain jobs) and higher order needs (e.g., multicultural awareness and diversity programming, counseling). Student affairs and faculty are probably similar on the collegiality-teamwork value; however, autonomy appears to be a much stronger value for faculty. The differences in the fourth value also reinforce for faculty the image of student affairs professionals as basic service providers.

Although faculty members and student affairs professionals have different values, assumptions, and responsibilities does not mean that they cannot work together or that conflict is inevitable. Clerical support personnel often have values and assumptions that differ from both faculty and student affairs professionals, yet most work effectively with both groups. There are other factors that contribute to the gap between faculty and student affairs professionals.

Perceptions of Each Other

How do faculty view student affairs professionals?

I was shocked to learn that several of the residence directors here have never been in a classroom, lecture hall, or the library on this campus. My faculty colleagues have vague and distorted ideas about what goes on beyond the classroom and in the residence halls, but many of the student life people are equally ignorant of the academic lives of the students in their charge. (Faculty member at a large state university on the east coast.)

This particular faculty member sees student affairs professionals as anti-intellectual. Moffatt (1989) provided an even more unflattering view of student affairs, based on his study of student culture at Rutgers University:

[Orientation] is the one institutional moment during which the student-life specialists. . . have a chance to tell *their* version of college to the freshmen, to try to represent Rutgers as a rational, well-ordered institution that cares about the individual student and. . . [their] personal development. Except that, as the deans themselves know, Rutgers is not really quite so caring, so orderly, or so personal.

> Accordingly, deanly orientation . . . was shot full of contradictions
> and double messages . . .
>
> The deans of students at Rutgers in the 1980s had [a] fragile sense
> of their own power . . . Like the British in India, the deans had their
> own loyal natives, their hundred or so preceptors [R.A.s], plus other
> students whose "personal development" they were "fostering" by
> co-opting them to their purposes. . . [T]he students hardly ever saw
> a dean in the flesh outside of orientation and the odd official func-
> tion. Consequently, most students led their college lives at Rutgers
> without thinking much about the deans at all (pp. 5, 36-37).

Moffatt portrayed the student affairs "deans" as untruthful, manipulative, blind, invisible, ineffective, and power-hungry. Con-
versely, many faculty are uninformed about the functions of student affairs professionals. Kuh et al. (1991) pointed out that even
at Involving Colleges, student affairs is a black box to many faculty, "a set of functions about which little is understood and even
less noticed" (p. 171). Student affairs professionals assert that they
make valuable contributions to the educational mission of their
institutions. Nevertheless, many faculty view themselves not only
as the core of the educational enterprise, but as the agents responsible for important educational outcomes.

Love (1990) proposed that conflict does not necessarily result
when two people or groups of people hold different values or assumptions. Conflict and frustration are more likely to result when
an individual or group *expects* values and assumptions to be similar, or when a group or individual assume others hold values and
assumptions that differ from their own. It can be argued that both
faculty and student affairs professionals agree on the values, assumptions, and tasks of faculty, but differ as to their views of the
values, assumptions and tasks of student affairs professionals, as
in the following statements.

> Faculty view the role of student affairs as: support service provid-
> ers; "fun and games" with students, not to be taken seriously; man-
> agers and administrators who are tangential to the educational mis-
> sion of the institution. Faculty view their own role as: autonomous;
> collegial; focused on teaching, research, service, and their discipline;
> and representing the core of the educational enterprise;
>
> Student affairs professionals view the role of faculty as: autono-
> mous; collegial; focused on teaching, research, service, and on the

discipline; but distant from student lives. Student affairs profession-als view their own role as: educators who administer (provide for both basic and higher order needs); focused on holistic student de-velopment; and complementing the academic mission of the institu-tion.

These descriptions suggest that faculty perceive student affairs functions to require little expertise, not as professional activities that demand knowledge about college student development and campus environments (National Association of Student Personnel Administrators, 1987).

Student affairs professionals often express frustration when they do not interact with faculty in ways that will help them better serve and educate students. To some extent, the unsatisfactory quality and frequency of relations with faculty on many campuses are due to fundamental differences in the way student affairs staff and fac-ulty view what student affairs professionals do. Key factors in addressing collaboration between student affairs professionals and faculty may include the size of the institution and its history and traditions. As Kuh et al. (1991) pointed out, faculty at large re-search institutions tend to be less involved with students outside the classroom even when their institution's history, traditions, and reward systems supported such behavior. Smaller, geographically isolated campuses with a liberal arts mission tend to be institutions in which involvement with students outside the classroom and, therefore, collaboration with student affairs, is not countercultural to faculty. The activities listed at the end of this chapter provide some ideas for overcoming cultural barriers to faculty and student affairs collaboration.

SUMMARY AND ACTIVITIES

The preceding sections may convey a less-than-optimistic tone about the prospects of developing effective working relationships with faculty. Each institution is unique; the cultures of both faculty and student affairs vary from institution to institution because both institution and discipline influence the values, beliefs, and assump-tions of both subcultures. Taking into account the cultures of fac-ulty and student affairs enriches understanding of both groups which increases the likelihood that student affairs and faculty can work together to create conditions that enhance student learning and development. While adopting a cultural view is not a guarantee for success, it will provide some answers about why faculty and student affairs professionals do not work as easily or well together as they can. That, in itself, is a worthwhile outcome.

Activities

The following suggestions are presented as a starting point to communicate across and work within the cultures of faculty and student affairs:

1. Get involved with academics. Join a committee, teach a class, take a class, attend a special lecture.

2. Get involved with faculty. Look for neutral ground to establish relationships (e.g., noon basketball games, morning or afternoon aerobics), take a class and get to know the professor, collaborate on research.

3. Personally invite faculty to be involved in one or more structured, day time, and time-limited tasks of student affairs (e.g., judicial boards, orientation planning committee, staff selection). They will probably learn much about the culture of the student affairs division and develop personal relationships with student affairs staff.

4. Recognize that faculty may not be as comfortable in the residence halls, dining hall, or other spaces designed for students as they are in their office or the classroom. Faculty with children in college may be more receptive to invitations to spend time with students as they sense firsthand the importance of out-of-class experiences in their own child's experience. Do what is necessary to make faculty comfortable, have a good experience, want to return and, perhaps, bring colleagues. This includes making certain that:

   a. Each program has at least some structured segment, so faculty will know what they will be doing and will have an opportunity to share some of their expertise or present on a favorite topic.

   b. Two or more faculty are present so that they feel comfortable in environments dominated by students.

   c. Faculty have an escort at all times (e.g., a student or the staff member coordinating the program), especially in the dining hall, to subtly show them what to do and to introduce them to students.

5. View every interaction with faculty as an opportunity to introduce them to the values and goals of your department and of the student affairs profession. Build an image where there is none and change the image where a negative one exists.

6. Follow through and have fun!

References

Aisenberg, N., & Harrington, M. (1988). *Women of academe: Outsiders in the sacred grove.* Amherst, MA: The University of Massachusetts Press.

Austin, A.E. (1990). Faculty cultures, faculty values. In W. Tierney (Ed.), *Assessing academic climates and cultures, New Directions for Institutional Research,* No. 68 (pp. 61–74). San Francisco: Jossey-Bass.

Austin, A.E., & Gamson, Z.F. (1983). *Academic workplace: New demands, heightened tensions.* ASHE-ERIC Higher Education Report, No. 10. Washington, D.C.: Association for the Study of Higher Education.

Baldridge, J.V., Curtis, D.V., Ecker, G., & Riley, G.L. (1978). *Policy making and effective leadership.* San Francisco: Jossey-Bass.

Becher, T. (1987). The cultural view. In B.R. Clark (Ed.), *Perspectives on higher education: Eight disciplinary and comparative views* (pp. 165–198). Berkeley and Los Angeles: University of California Press.

Bess, J.L. (1982). *University organization: A matrix analysis of the academic professions.* New York: Human Services Press.

Blau, P.M. (1973). *The organization of academic work.* New York: Wiley.

Bowen, H.R., & Schuster, J.H. (1986). *American professors.* Oxford: Oxford University Press.

Boyer, E.L. (1987). *College: The undergraduate experience in America.* New York: Harper & Row.

Chamberlain, M.K. (1988). *Women in academe: Progress and prospects.* New York: Russell Sage Foundation.

Clark, B.R. (1963). Faculty culture. In T.F. Lunsford (Ed.), *The study of campus cultures* (pp. 39–51). Boulder, CO: Western Interstate Commission on Higher Education.

Clark, B.R. (1984). *The higher education system: Academic organization in cross–national perspective.* Berkeley and Los Angeles: University of California Press.

Dill, D.D. (1982). The management of academic culture: Notes on the management of meaning and social integration. *Higher Education, 11,* 303–20.

Eickmann, P.E. (1988). *Teaching values by example: Let's examine the profession's personal values.* Paper presented at the annual meeting of the College Student Personnel Association of New York State, Rochester, NY.

Freedman, M.B. (1979). *Academic culture and faculty development.* Berkeley, CA: Montaigne.

Gerson, K. (1985). *Hard choices: How women decide about work, career, and motherhood,* Berkeley, CA: University of California Press.

Goffigon, R., Wright, J., Lacey, D., & Kuh, G.D. (1986). The small college experience: The generalist's perspective. In G.D. Kuh and A.C. McAleenan (Eds.) *Private dreams, shared visions: Student affairs work in small colleges* (pp. 95–104). Washington, D.C.: National Association of Student Personnel Administrators.

Gouldner, A.W. (1957). Cosmopolitans and locals. *Administrative Science Quarterly, 2,* 281–306, 444–80.

Hochschild, A. (1989). *Second shift.* Berkeley, CA: University of California Press.

Kitchner, K.S. (1985). Ethical principles and ethical decisions in student affairs. In H.J. Canon and R.D. Brown (Eds.), *Applied ethics in student services, New Directions for Student Services,* No. 30 (pp. 7–30). San Francisco: Jossey-Bass.

Kuh, G.D., & Schuh, J.H. (Eds.) (1991). *The role and contributions of student affairs in Involving Colleges.* Washington, D.C.: National Association of Student Personnel Administrators.

Kuh, G.D., Schuh, J.H., Whitt, E.J., & Associates (1991). *Involving colleges: Successful approaches to fostering student learn-*

ing and development outside the classroom. San Francisco: Jossey-Bass.

Kuh, G.D., Shedd, J.D., & Whitt, E.J. (1987). Student affairs and liberal education: Unrecognized (and unappreciated) common law partners. *Journal of College Student Personnel, 28,* 252–260.

Kuh, G.D., & Whitt, E.J. (1988). *The invisible tapestry: Culture in American colleges and universities.* ASHE-ERIC Higher Education Report, No. 1. Washington, D.C.: Association for the Study of Higher Education.

Kuh, G.D., Whitt, E.J., & Shedd, J.D. (1987). *Student affairs, 2001: A paradigmatic odyssey.* Alexandria, VA: American College Personnel Association.

Ladd, E.C., & Lipset, S.M. (1975–76). The Ladd-Lipset Survey. *Chronicle of Higher Education, 11*(7) p 2, *11*(8) p 2.

Light, D. (1974). Introduction: The structure of academic professions. *Sociology of Education, 47* (1), 2–28.

Love, P.G. (1990). *An investigation into the organizational culture of a student affairs department.* Unpublished doctoral dissertation. Indiana University, Bloomington, IN.

McAleenan, A.C., & Kuh, G.D. (1986). The context for student affairs work in small colleges. In G.D. Kuh and A.C. McAleenan (Eds.), *Private dreams, shared visions: Student affairs work in small colleges* (pp. 1–10). Washington, D.C.: National Association of Student Personnel Administrators.

Metzger, W.P. (1987). The academic profession in the United States. In B.R. Clark (Ed.), *The academic profession* (pp. 123–208). Berkeley and Los Angeles: University of California Press.

Mills, M.R. (1987). *Pursuing cultural change: An organization fends for itself.* Paper presents at the annual meeting of the Association for the Study of Higher Education, Baltimore, MD.

Moffatt, M. (1988). *Coming of age in New Jersey: College and American culture.* New Brunswick, NJ: Rutgers University Press.

Morrill, P.H., & Spees, E.R. (1982). *The academic profession: Teaching in higher education.* New York: Human Sciences Press.

Pearson, C.S., Shavlik, D.L., & Touchton, J.G. (1988). *Educating the majority: Women challenge tradition in higher education.* New York: American Council on Education.

Ruscio, K.P. (1987). Many sectors, many professions. In B.R. Clark (Ed.), *The academic profession: National, disciplinary, and institutional settings* (pp. 331–368). Berkeley and Los Angeles: University of California Press.

Stamatakos, L.C. (1981). Student affairs progress toward professionalism: Recommendations for action, part 1. *Journal of College Student Personnel, 22,* 105–113. (a)

Stamatakos, L.C. (1981). Student affairs progress toward professionalism: Recommendations for action, part 2. *Journal of College Student Personnel, 22,* 197–207. (b)

Stamatakos, L.C., & Rogers, R. (1984). Student affairs: A profession in need of a philosophy. *Journal of College Student Personnel, 25,* 400–411.

Van Maanen, J. (1984). Doing new things in old ways: The chains of socialization. In J. L. Bess (Ed.), *College and university organization: Insights from the behavioral sciences* (pp. 211–247). New York: New York University Press.

Whitt, E.J. (1988). *Hit the ground running: Experiences of new faculty in the school of education at a research university.* Unpublished doctoral dissertation. Indiana University, Bloomington, IN.

Winston, R.B., & Saunders, S.A. (1991). Ethical practice in student affairs. In T.K. Miller & R.B. Winston (eds.) *Administration and leadership in student affairs: Actualizing student development in higher education* (pp. 309–346). Muncie, IN: Accelerated Development.

CHAPTER 4

Student Culture

Patrick G. Love
Victor J. Boschini
Bruce A. Jacobs
Christine M. Hardy
George D. Kuh

Efforts on the part of institutions of higher education and national Greek organizations have not eliminated hazing, alcohol abuse, and sexual harassment within the fraternity system.

Colleges and universities successful in attracting increasing numbers of students from historically underrepresented racial and ethnic groups find that increased cultural diversity brings with it new problems and new tensions.

The Nelligan Hall "Pit," a residence hall floor at Le Moyne College, annually generates more discipline sanctions and sustains more damages resulting from vandalism than any other residence hall floor on campus.

Resident assistants on many campuses bemoan the lack of response to their educational programming efforts; "students," they say, "just won't come."

Recall that Chapter One also began with a list of problems faced by most colleges and universities in the United States. The above examples identify matters related to student culture that require attention by student affairs professionals.

Student culture exerts a significant influence on many aspects of college life (Baird, 1988; Weidman, 1989). Students become connected to their institution through the groups with which they affiliate and identify (Tinto, 1987). Knowing with what groups students primarily identify helps determine where students fit in the overall student culture. Students who identify with marginal or loosely connected groups (e.g., commuters on a residential campus) usually feel less connected to the overall student culture; those who feel unconnected are less likely to graduate (Tinto, 1987). Equally important, "student cultures offer their members thick and thin guidelines for how to get an education and thus define for students just what an education means" (Van Maanen, 1987, p. 5).

Admonitions regarding the inherent complexity of culture were delineated in Chapter One and warrant repeating here. Before student cultures can be influenced, they must first be identified and understood. Given the variety of groups, experiences, and individual values and beliefs that exist in a typical institution of higher education—even a small, college with a relatively homogeneous student body—student affairs professionals cannot possible understand all the cultural dynamics at work in their institution. However, with a healthy respect for this complexity and an openness to learning more about their institution, using cultural perspectives can greatly increase a student affairs professional's knowledge of students and their experiences. Practitioners who are knowledgeable about and understand the various student cultures on their campus are better positioned to create campus environments that foster student learning and personal development.

The purpose of this chapter is to illustrate how using cultural perspectives can lead to a better understanding and appreciation for students—their groups, their activities, and their behaviors. National, institutional, and intra-institutional levels of student culture are identified and discussed. Then, how student cultures develop and change are addressed. Finally, implications for student affairs practitioners are considered.

LEVELS OF STUDENT CULTURE

Using the "student body" as the unit of analysis for examining student culture obfuscates the considerable heterogeneity in students' backgrounds, behaviors, attitudes, and beliefs. Every college's student body is made up of such varied groups as classes, majors, roommates, suitemates, floors, residence halls, intramural teams, varsity sports teams, clubs, organizations, social groups (e.g., fraternities, sororities), study groups, honor societies, and paraprofessionals. By studying these groups and their activities from cultural perspectives student affairs practitioners can learn how various groups contribute to or detract from the campus community, why some students and groups are successful while others are unsuccessful, and why some students are satisfied and others dissatisfied with their collegiate experience.

It should not be surprising, given the complexity of the concept, that student culture has multiple levels. Chapter One identified one set of levels (artifacts, perspectives, values, assumptions). Another set of levels is presented in this section: national, institutional, and intra-institutional aspects of student culture (Kuh, 1990). Key to using these particular levels of student culture is identifying the artifacts, perspectives, values, and assumptions that students share at each level.

National Level

According to Becker (1961), student culture on all campuses is similar in some respects. For example, despite differences in age, ethnicity, socio-economic status, and educational background, college students face the same basic challenges, such as choosing a major, becoming acquainted with the campus environment, adjusting to people from different backgrounds, and learning how the institution works (e.g., registration, drop and add). Most traditional-age students must master certain developmental tasks—becoming independent from parents and achieving full adult status in a world in which they often are treated as children (Newcomb & Wilson, 1966). These common tasks create a sense of shared experience among undergraduate student cohorts, even for students at institutions many hundreds of miles apart. Indeed, student culture *is* the experience of being a college student.

In this sense, it is not surprising that national surveys often produce views of students as a unitary group, with shared perspectives, values, and assumptions. For example, according to Astin (1985), entering college students in the 1980s were more materialistic and self-interested than were their counterparts in the 1960s and 1970s. The career-oriented values of the student culture that characterized students in the late 1970s and 1980s (Astin, 1985) were attributed, in part, to changes in the types of students attending college, especially part-timers and returning women students. Recent research (Levine & Hirsh, 1990) has indicated that students of the 1990s may be shifting to more other-centered values. This conclusion is based on an increased interest in volunteerism, a decrease in the number of students choosing business majors, an increase in students majoring in more service-oriented majors (e.g., education), and an increase in those seeking more socially mean- ingful jobs. Also, the presence of increasing numbers of students of color have influenced the values and assumptions of contempo- rary college student culture.

National (Horowitz, 1987) and multi-institutional portraits (Astin, 1985) of student culture provide information about shifting student moods, attitudes, and values. These descriptions can be used to test assumptions about students at a given campus. For example, if—as the data from the Cooperative Institutional Research Program (Astin, 1985) suggested—volunteerism is on the rise, then student affairs professionals should attempt to capitalize on this trend at their own institution by forging relations with agencies in nearly communities to create outlets for students to express their interest.

Institutional Level

Just as institutional cultures are unique, so, too, are student cul- tures. In part, this is due to differences in the values and attitudes of students who attend different types of institutions. For example, Astin (1965) determined that intellectualism and pragmatism were significantly more important values for students entering techno- logical institutions than for students entering other institutions. Status was considered important by students at private liberal arts colleges.

According to Kuh (1990):

> When examined at the institutional level, the characteristics of student cultures may differ markedly from those apparent at the national level. For example, the attitudes at Earlham College, a Quaker institution, are the converse of those reflected by CIRP data, which show that increasing proportions of entering college students want to earn a lot of money after college while decreasing propor- tions expect to develop a meaningful philosophy of life. Special mission institutions, such as military academies, engineering and technical colleges, and institutions with a pervasive religious orien- tation (for example, Barry College and Bob Jones University), at-

tract students with relatively homogeneous attitudes that are congruent with these institutions' philosophies and educational purposes (pp. 48-49).

Discovering what is important to students at a particular college or university can help in identifying salient aspects of the student culture. New students learn what is important through their interactions with current students as well as new student orientation. Students teach each other about "gut" courses, the drop/add process, "proper" modes of dress and activities, and how to communicate with administrators and faculty (Van Maanen, 1987). Through "terms of endearment" (Kuh, et al., 1991), students new to Le Moyne College discover that "hooking" with another student means you have spontaneously connected with a student of the opposite sex (see also Durst & Schaeffer, 1992), or that at Miami University of Ohio "Miami mergers" are marriages between two Miami students.

On occasion, institutional traditions communicate these understandings—Big May Day at Earlham College, Dolphy Day at Le Moyne College, Fountain Day at The University at Albany, Labor Day at Berea College, Founder's Day at Xavier University of New Orleans, and Little 500 Weekend at Indiana University. Some of these traditions reinforce institutional values and priorities, others conflict with them; but through sharing these experiences they all connect students to the institution. Other more traditional activities such as new student orientation, convocation, homecoming, and commencement also contribute to the development of the sense of belonging to the institution as a greater entity.

There is, however, a danger in viewing student culture as monolithic. In many cases, the differences in perspectives, values, and assumptions of student groups within institutions far outweigh the similarities, the topic to which we now turn.

Intra-institutional Level

In his study of the culture at Vassar College, Bushnell (1962) determined that the student body, faculty, administration, and graduate students were differentiated subcultures; while all of these groups combined to create the overall culture that is Vassar College, they also represented individual subcultures. The differentiated student groups that make up the student body vary in cultural strength. That is, the members of some groups exhibit certain cultural characteristics (e.g., shared perspectives, values, assumptions) or hold values and assumptions different from the overall student body or institution. Some groups are transient (e.g., a floor in a residence hall) and have few shared experiences or values required to become distinctive subculture. The number and strength of groups depend on the size of the institution; that is, more groups exist in large institutions of higher education, fewer in smaller colleges with homogeneous student bodies. Because the values, goals, and assumptions of these groups may vary widely from each other and from those of the student body at large, very different perceptions of the institution can result (Baird, 1988; Pace & Baird, 1966). So, as Kuh (1990) indicated, "just as national data can be misleading when applied to a specific institution, data aggregated at the institutional level can obscure the variation in attitudes and behaviors of different student groups" (p. 49).

Three types of groups found at most institutions will be discussed in this section: (a) subcultures; (b) peer, reference, and affinity groups (including time or location specific groups); and (c) culturally-marginalized groups. Various student groups may fit more than one category and, given that culture is constantly evolving, groups will move from one category to another, according to fluctuations in numbers of members and the degree to which the group influences its members behavior.

Subcultures. A subculture has beliefs, norms, and practices distinctive enough to distinguish it from other groups within the same institution (Sergiovani, 1984). Bolton and Kammeyer (1972, pp. 381-382) further defined a subculture as a "normative-value system held by some group of persons who are in persisting interaction, who transmit the norms and values to newcomers by some communicational process and who exercise some sort of social control to ensure conformity to the norms."

One of the common denominators for development of a student subculture is a common living area (e.g., sorority and fraternity houses, athletic dorms). A common living area insures propinquity (i.e., students who live in close proximity and, thus, see each other regularly), and encourages active sharing and continuous, persisting interaction among members. Propinquity and persistent interaction are, as will be discussed later, important to the emergence of a peer group or subculture. For example, International House at

Le Moyne College, founded 25 years ago by Daniel Berrigan, evolved from a club into a subculture when members began to live together in a house on campus. To heighten student's awareness of national and international problems and cultures, members of the organization were encouraged to work for at least one week per year in Mexico or Central America (this has since shifted to Appalachia and the inner-city). These group experiences helped to shape the early mission and ideals of the organization. Several times each year other members of the campus community are invited to "IH dinners" where the International House's history and traditions are renewed through a slide show which reviews the organization's history and the telling of stories.

Perhaps the clearest example of a student subculture are Greek-letter systems on most campuses. Fraternities began as social clubs; over the years they developed to the point where many meet the most stringent definition of a subculture. Fraternity members often live together and are, therefore, in "persisting interaction." They transmit the group's norms and values through the rituals of pledging and induction, and exercise a great deal of control—both informal (e.g., peer pressure, threats) and formal (e.g., rules and policies)—over the behavior of members (Leemon, 1972). The culture of the fraternity often is so strong that systematic efforts by administrators to eliminate hazing and reduce instances of alcohol abuse and sexual harassment and abuse have been, for the most part, unsuccessful (Arnold & Kuh, 1992). As a result, the values of some fraternities often are in conflict with the institution's values; that is, these groups have become counter-cultural (Chapter 1).

Other examples of student subcultures might include Black Greek organizations, athletic teams (especially those where students reside in athletic dormitories, receive special privileges, share meals), and long-established residence-based organizations (e.g., Collins Living-Learning Center at Indiana University, Western College at Miami University of Ohio).

Studies of student subcultures in the 1960s did not define subcultures in the way that they are being defined here. A more accurate label of the product of that research was the development of student typologies, a framework with multiple categories which describes *types* of students, not subcultures. Student typologies were devised by Newcomb, Koenig, Flacks, and Warwick (1967), Keniston (1965), and Katchadourian and Boli (1985). Perhaps the best-known typology is that of Clark and Trow (1966) who identified four college student "subcultures": academic, collegiate, vocational, and nonconformist. Whereas Clark and Trow's typology provided a heuristic framework for exploring some student characteristics, their four categories do not meet the definition of a subculture or peer group outlined in this chapter. For example, students categorized in the Clark-Trow "subcultures" do not persistently interact, do not necessarily actively share experiences, nor do they exert social control over each other. Bolton and Kammeyer (1972) maintained that Clark and Trow described role orientations of students rather than a subculture. Kuh (1990) discussed in more depth the issue of role orientations and their relationship to subcultures.

Peer groups. The term "peer group" also encompasses reference and affinity groups. A peer group is an associational group (Morrill, Hurst & Associates, 1980) with which a student identifies, interacts, and derives a frame of reference for evaluating personal attitudes, values, and behaviors (Upcraft & Pilato, 1982). Some peer groups are time or location-specific. Such groups tend to be less formal than the groups mentioned earlier and are transient (e.g., new or one-time clubs, most residence hall floors).

An example of a continuing peer or associational group is the "Pit" at Le Moyne College, which is the first floor of Nelligan Hall. It is called the "Pit" because one must walk down stairs to reach it and the ceilings of the rooms are much higher than on other floors. Over time, however, the name, "the Pit," has taken on a pejorative connotation as traditions developed to express disrespect for both the facilities and the residence life staff. There is a high degree of student turnover on the Pit from year to year; yet the reputation and tradition of the floor are well known. As a result, students with certain attitudes choose to live there; thus, discipline problems and high rates of damage and vandalism persist.

Whereas the "Pit" is a continuing problem, many residence life professionals have experienced the seemingly spontaneous emergence of a "renegade" floor that requires strong disciplinary responses from student life staff. The coming together of students with a combination of certain expectations, values and assumptions sets in motion the development of a peer group with behaviors and attitudes that are antithetical to the institution's values. Other combinations of students' characteristics foster the development of "wonder floors" where there is a high degree of student involvement and participation, and students identify with institutional values and relate well to each other. The class year group (e.g., Class of '91) is another possible peer group. The influence of the class year group on student values varies in strength from institution to institution, but seems to be especially strong in smaller, residential institutions where it is possible for individuals to know and develop relationships with a greater percentage of the class than would be possible at a school with a graduating class of several thousands. Strong class year influence is evident at military academies where cohort identity remains important throughout military careers. Other peer groups include some athletic teams, intramural teams, and academic major groups that have relatively few members and, therefore, a high degree of interaction (e.g., theater). There also are many informal groups on campus that are not easy to label, including friendship groups (Morrill, Hurst and Associates, 1980), that develop over time and persist beyond separation from the institution.

If members of a peer group stay together over a long period of time, and if the group is able to pass on norms, values, and traditions to its members from year to year, then the group may develop into a subculture. In that sense, a subculture is a peer group; however, given its capacity to exercise control and transmit norms and values that meet long-term group maintenance needs, the typical subculture has a longer life span than peer or associational groups. Most student government organizations, student orientation committees, and resident advisor staffs qualify as peer groups and not subcultures. That is, even though they exist year after year, they are not subcultures because their members do not share norms and values, or there is not a pervasive sense of group history, or the groups exert relatively little social control over the behavior of members.

Culturally marginalized groups. Depending on the campus, these groups might include any of the following: physically challenged students, international students, older students, commuter students, women at military institutions, and students of color. Whereas members of peer groups and subcultures feel they are a part of the institution—even if their values and assumptions are countercultural—students in culturally marginalized groups feel disconnected from the institution, express less satisfaction with their experience and, therefore, are less likely to stay in school

(Pascarella & Terenzini, 1991, Tinto, 1987). Schlossberg (1989) suggested that people need to feel that they matter, that their input is valued, and that they are a part of the organization. When people do not feel as though they matter, or when they do not share experiences with other members of the organization, or when they do not share values and assumptions similar to those of other members of the organization (or do not even know what those values and assumptions are), they view themselves as marginal. Marginality also can exist when people change roles or join a new organization.

On many campuses, the attitudes and expectations of commuter students of traditional age may not differ from those of residence students (Chickering, 1974). However, because they do not live on campus, they feel unconnected to the campus and to each other. Commuter students tend to have less contact with faculty, fewer close friends at the college, and are less likely to participate in extracurricular activities and take part in intellectual discussions (Chickering, 1974). These are the very behaviors that socialize resident students and connect them to the campus. Commuter students are not so much a marginalized group, but marginalized individuals, because they rarely have an identity as a group.

Whereas some marginalized individuals may not feel part of a group, students of color can feel a strong sense of group membership, yet still feel marginal as far as the institution is concerned. Student of color organizations (e.g., AHANA—African, Hispanic, Asian, Native American—groups, a multicultural society, Black Student Union) organize support groups based on race or ethnicity. Through the group, members develop a sense of shared experience and develop ways of coping with the dominant culture. Separation from the institution, however, can have negative consequences for marginal groups, and foster a feeling of marginality for the organization and its members, a sense that they do not matter to the institution (Goldberg, 1941). This feeling can sometimes result in higher dropout rates than members of the dominant culture:

> Black students on white campuses reportedly experienced consider-
> able difficulty adjusting to a culturally different, academically
> demanding, and socially alienating environment. As a result . . .
> black students on these campuses do not experience reasonable lev-
> els of academic success and college satisfaction [and have] higher
> attrition rates (Allen, 1987, p. 28).

DYNAMICS OF STUDENT CULTURE

In this section, the dynamics of peer group and subculture development are considered in more detail. Attention is given to the precollegiate and college-based characteristics of students in peer group formation, factors related to group persistence, and the relationship of these subgroups to the overall student culture.

Peer Group Formation

Peer group formation at the collegiate level results from many factors, including precollegiate and group-based considerations. Precollegiate factors are those that existed before coming to college, such as acquaintanceship prior to college, age, gender, social class, religious affiliation, aspirations, and goals (Newcomb, 1962). Newcomb and Wilson (1966) pointed out that "there are many institutions of higher education . . . whose policies of admission together with their selective drawing power result in both attitudinal homogeneity and communicative isolation (p. 14). That is, the student's selection of college and the college's selection of students tend to reduce the variance in precollegiate factors that exist in the student body. For example, The Evergreen State College, an alternative liberal arts college in Washington, tends to attract students who have more liberal attitudes than students at Brigham Young University which is known for conservative policies.

College-based factors of peer group formation include propinquity (e.g., students who are placed together in a residence hall or students who share several classes), choice of academic major, and membership in clubs and organizations.

> Affiliations sought in college are affected by students' educational backgrounds, socioeconomic status, political and religious beliefs, goals for the college experiences, and psychological characteristics and needs. Students who live near one another, who attend class together, or who are isolated from non-students are more likely to meet and have opportunities for reciprocal exploration (Kuh & Whitt, 1988, p. 87).

Newcomb (1961) reported that interpersonal attraction and the frequency of association were related to the number of issues about which the individuals were in agreement. Certain groups within institutions, such as fraternities and sororities, typically draw their members from higher socioeconomic backgrounds (Feldman & Newcomb, 1969), thus creating groups of members with homogeneous characteristics. Newcomb and Wilson (1966) reported that the need among traditional college students for acceptance by same-age and same-gender peers contributed to the rate of peer group development and the strength of the bonds among members. "Many students describe themselves as lonely and isolated during their first weeks or months at college . . . Such feelings of isolation can lead to a strong drive to be affiliated with, and dependent on, other students" (LeVine, 1966, p. 119). Given these factors, the college campus, especially for first-year students and for those who live in residence halls, is an environment rich with opportunities and encouragements for peer group formation.

Group Persistence and Strength

Once a peer group is established, it begins to influence the behavior and attitudes of group members and those who seek to affiliate with the group (Newcomb, 1962). The influence of a peer group on its members is increased when: (a) the size of the institution is large and the group has a relatively small number of members, (b) members' attitudes and interests are homogeneous, (c) membership in the group is viewed as important by participants, and (d) members are relatively isolated with regard to opportunities for frequent interaction with group outsiders (Newcomb, 1962). Thus, at an institution with many thousands of students, a fraternity tends to have more influence on its members than a residence hall floor due to the relative importance of membership for the members of the fraternity as compared to members of a residence hall floor, particularly if the fraternity is physically isolated from other groups (e.g., has its own house on the edge of campus).

Whether a group will persist over time depends on the discovery or development of similar interests and similar attitudes and intentions (Newcomb, 1962) and the degree of fact to face interaction. Continuous interaction within an isolated group produces the understandings and attitudes that form the basis of student culture (Hughes, Becker & Geer, 1962). Students within an interacting group tend to shape each other's values and attitudes; the more they interact the more they begin to resemble each other in terms of values and attitudes. Feldman and Newcomb (1969) reported that students who lived on residence hall floors where their major field of study was different from most other students tended to change their major more often than those in the majority. This "progressive conformity" resulted in students changing their major to one of the dominant majors represented on the floor.

Frequent face-to-face interaction encourages the development of shared meanings and interpretations of experience (Love, 1990). Active sharing highlights individual interpretations and commonalities; when differences are discussed, they may be diluted, allowing individuals to develop alternative frameworks with which to interpret future events and experiences. Once a framework is developed, it tends to be reinforced rather than challenged by future experiences. One of the reasons that the fraternity cultures are so strong is that the pledge process provides for a high degree of active sharing that develops very common and highly reinforced frameworks of interpretation for new members (Arnold & Kuh, 1992; Leemon, 1972). If the institution's administration is viewed as the enemy by the fraternity, each encounter by members of the fraternity with members of the administration is filtered through that framework. Given a negative view of the administration, "attacks" by the administration on student behavior (e.g., enforcement of alcohol policy) reinforce the framework and "encouraging" behaviors (e.g., leadership training) are either discounted or interpreted as manipulative behaviors or attempts at co-opting the group.

Peer Group and Subculture Evolution and Change

Efforts to systematically change or influence student culture are difficult to implement successfully, due to the interaction among the many factors that influence the development of culture. As discussed in Chapter 7, Those attempting to change student culture, subcultures, or peer groups should bear in mind this complexity.

At the same time, culture is not stagnant; it is a dynamic process of development, evolution, renewal, decline, and demise. Tierney (1987) asserted that cultural groups acquire and lose power due to the constantly shifting nature of the organizations and their participants. Even if there is a strong socialization process, given the mutually shaping nature of culture, new members will change the group as well as be changed by the group. Clubs and organizations on campus change from year to year because of the changing composition of their members and leaders. Thus, peer groups and subcultures are continually changing, albeit at times in ways that are imperceptible (Tierney, 1987).

Some factors that influence cultural change have been mentioned already, including the introduction of such new and different students into institutions of higher education as women, veterans, people of color, and returning and older students. The very presence of these groups influences the overall student culture. An important step in attempts to modify student culture is to identify and discuss openly the tacit aspects of a group's culture—its values, assumptions, and interpretive frameworks (Love, 1990). "It is sometimes easier to change the attitudes of an entire group than of a single individual" (Lewin in Newcomb & Wilson, 1966, p. 13). By discovering the assumptions upon which the group's behavior is based, the group can choose to change their behavior and reinforce new attitudes and actions. Therefore, group support can be mobilized *for* change as well as against it. So, the most direct way to influence the culture of a group is to change the characteristics of its members.

Isolation contributes to the development of groups with strongly held values and attitudes. Communicative isolation is more influential than physical isolation in modifying behavior (Newcomb & Wilson, 1966). Therefore, breaking down the isolation between two groups or subcultures (e.g., divergent student organizations, students and faculty, fraternities and the administration) may modify attitudes and norms that, in turn, may change the differences between the two groups. Moving physically isolated groups (e.g., deviant residence hall floors, student of color organizations) closer to the academic core of a campus can increase their communication and interaction with other groups and also lead to a change in an isolated group's attitudes and experiences. Isolating a group, such as assigning new students from dominant campus cultures to residence halls on the edge of campus creates opportunities for the group to develop its own attitudes and norms, rather than adopting those of the dominant student culture.

Students and their cultures *can* and *will* change, but there is no sure-fire, systematic way of controlling the change or predicting what the change will be. Therefore, formal change attempts should be tentative and flexible. Attempts to positively influence student culture are treated in more depth in Chapter 6.

IMPLICATIONS FOR STUDENT AFFAIRS PROFESSIONALS

In this section, implications and suggestions are offered for student affairs professionals attempting to understand culture and enhance student learning and personal development.

1. *Know thyself.*

A prerequisite for understanding student culture is to discover and understand your own values and assumptions. Identify the values that guide your behavior, the assumptions you hold, and the frameworks you use in dealing with students. Reflect on how you came to hold your beliefs, values, and assumptions. Ask others what they believe to be your values and assumptions. Are they different from your own?

2. *Discover the various student cultures on campus.*

Most students learn from peers how to communicate with faculty and administrators. They will tend to use faculty and administrative language and address the values faculty and administrators espouse. It is important to get beyond the boundaries between the two cultures to discover the values and assumptions that students hold and the frameworks they use to negotiate their lives as students. Seek to know their cultures from their perspective. Develop the ability to listen to students while screening out your assumptions and frames of reference.

3. *Use cultural perspectives for diagnosis and analysis.*

As stated earlier, before attempting to change something about a group of students is important to first understand it. Study both deviant "renegade" groups and extraordinary "wonder" groups from cultural perspectives. What artifacts are associated with these groups (e.g., history, traditions, rituals, stories, heroes and heroines)? What are the forces (e.g., a tragedy, some common experience) and factors (e.g., age, gender, residence hall, shared values) that brought these people together as a group and what has happened culturally (i.e., persistent interaction, development of norms, shared experiences) to keep them together? What are the values and assumptions common to the members of this group?

4. *Recognize the importance of living areas and affinity groups to student culture.*

Propinquity and persisting interaction are strong factors in the development of culture. Providing living areas for certain groups is one way to shape the culture development process. Recall that a common living area contributed to the emergence of the enhancing International House subculture at Le Moyne College. Removing members from a problem living area also is a tactic for breaking up a counter-cultural subgroup. Some institutions have banned fraternities after failing to change their behavior. One way to respond to a residence floor that has developed a dysfunctional culture (e.g., high rates of vandalism and policy violation, lack of respect for the institution or other students) is to "break up the floor" and move its members to other parts of campus. This action usually destroys the sense of group, by diluting the values and norms among other student groups and cultures.

5. *Be wary of attempts to systematically change student cultures, but recognize that student cultures can be changed.*

Systematic attempts to change student culture are likely to fall short. However, student culture can be influenced. Consider an institution with a student culture with assumptions and values that are antithetical to the institution's aims. One step is to investigate from the students' perspective how this anti-institutional mindset developed. To change these aspects of the student culture the administration can start with the incoming class and attempt to counter the socialization by current students by bringing in new students before other students return. Depending on the institution, other possible interventions include preparing student orientation leaders to recognize the influence they have on the first year students, clearly articulating institutional values to the new class through programs, publications, and other media, and having residences for first year students. Campus leaders must recognize that there is no way to accurately predict the outcome of such an effort, but by understanding the processes of culture development on campus, the institution can take steps to try to counter them.

6. *Use cultural perspectives when working with marginal groups.*

a. Find ways to ensure that members feel they "matter" (e.g., solicit their input in institutional matters, involve staff with different groups of students, do not assign only professionals of color to work with students of color);

b. Develop ways for students to actively share and persistently interact with others, such as establishing and maintaining a commuter lounge; and

c. Enhance students' status in groups other than their "marginal" group (e.g., expect and encourage commuters to join clubs or organizations as part of their graduation requirements, recruit students of color to participate in and help develop residence hall programming).

SUMMARY AND ACTIVITIES

How student cultures influence student learning and personal development has been of interest for many decades. Student affairs professionals work with students both as individuals and in groups. It is imperative that student affairs professionals recognize the influence subcultures, peer, and affinity groups have on their members.

Activities

The following activities are designed to help student affairs professionals gain a richer appreciation for the student cultures that exist on their campus.

1. Go to a residence hall (not your own if you are a hall director) between 7:00 p.m. and 9:00 p.m. on a week night. Wear casual clothes. Engage a small group of students in a conversation, explain what you are doing, and ask some of the following questions:
   a. What does it mean to be a student at this institution?
   b. What are the various associational or affinity groups to which the students belong? With what groups do they primarily identify? What does it mean to be a member of each of these groups? How are the groups and the members of the groups different from each other?
   c. What are the students' views of faculty and administration? What do the students perceive to be the goals and values of the faculty and administration?
   d. What are the conventions of attire, language, and socializing for students? How does one know if they "fit in?"
   e. What are the best and worst aspects of being a student at the institution?
2. Repeat the above with some of the following groups or in some of the following places:
   a. students in the commuter lounge;
   b. members of a group based on race or ethnicity;

c. a fraternity or sorority house;
d. a theater group;
e. members of the student government; and
f. students who stand out as being different from the norm due to dress, reputation, attitude, or achievement (high or low).
3. Answer the following questions:
   a. What have you learned about the institution's student culture and students in general?
   b. What have you learned about your own perspectives, values, and assumptions?
   c. How many different groups were you able to identify? What are the attributes, traits, and factors which differentiate the groups?

REFERENCES

Allen, W.R. (1987). Black colleges vs. White colleges: The fork in the road for Black students. *Change, 19*(3), 28–34.

Arnold, J.C., & Kuh, G.D. (1992, March). *Brotherhood over the bottle: A cultural analysis of the role of alcohol in fraternities.* Bloomington, IN: The Center for the Study of the College Fraternity.

Astin, A.W. (1965). *Who goes where to college?* Chicago: SRA.

Astin, A.W. (1985). *Achieving educational excellence: A critical assessment of priorities and practices in higher education.* San Francisco: Jossey-Bass.

Baird, L.L. (1988). The college environment revisited: A review of research and theory. In J.C. Smart (Ed.), *Higher education: Handbook of theory and research*, Vol. 4 (pp. 1–52). New York: Agathon.

Becker, H.S., Geer, B., Hughes, E.C., & Strauss, A.L. (1961). *Boys in white: Student culture in medical school.* Chicago: University of Chicago Press.

Bolton, C.D., & Kammeyer, K.C.W. (1972). Campus cultures, role orientations, and social types. In K.A. Feldman (Ed.), *College and student: Selected readings in the social psychology of higher education* (pp. 377–391). Elmsford, NY: Pergamon.

Bushnell, J. (1962). Student culture at Vassar. In N. Sanford (Ed.), *The American College: A psychological and social interpretation of the higher learning* (pp. 489–514). New York: Wiley.

Chickering, A.W. (1974). *Commuting versus resident students: Overcoming the educational inequities of living off campus.* Jossey-Bass: San Francisco.

Clark, B.R., & Trow, M. (1966). The organizational context. In T.M. Newcomb and E.K. Wilson (Eds.), *College peer groups: Problems and prospects for research* (pp. 17–70). Chicago: Aldine.

Durst, M., & Schaeffer, E.M. (1992). *A cultural analysis of student life at a liberal arts college.* Lewiston, NY: Edwin Mellen.

Feldman, K.A., & Newcomb, T.M. (1969). *The impact of college on students.* San Francisco: Jossey-Bass.

Goldberg, M.M. (1941). A qualification of the marginal man theory. *American Sociological Review, 6,* 52–58.

Horowitz, H.L. (1987). *Campus life: Undergraduate cultures from the end of the eighteenth century to the present.* New York: Knopf.

Hughes, E.C., Becker, H.S., & Geer, B. (1962). Student culture and academic effort. In N. Sanford (Ed.), *The American college: A psychological and social interpretation of the higher learning* (pp. 515–530). New York: Wiley.

Katchadourian, H.A., & Boli, J. (1985). *Careerism and intellectualism among college students: Patterns of academic and career choice in the undergraduate years.* San Francisco: Jossey-Bass.

Keniston, K. (1965). *The uncommitted: Alienated youth in American society.* San Diego, CA: Harcourt Brace Jovanovich.

Kuh, G.D. (1990). Assessing student culture. In W. Tierney (Ed.), *Assessing academic climates and cultures, New Directions for Institutional Research,* No. 68 (pp. 47–60). San Francisco: Jossey-Bass.

Kuh, G.D., Schuh, J.H., Whitt, E.J. & Associates (1991). *Involving colleges: Successful approaches to fostering student learning and development outside the classroom.* San Francisco: Jossey-Bass.

Kuh, G.D., & Whitt, E.J. (1988). *The invisible tapestry: Culture in American colleges and universities.* ASHE-ERIC Higher Education Report, No. 1. Washington, DC: Association for the Study of Higher Education.

Leemon, T.A. (1972). *The rites of passage in a student culture.* New York: Teachers College Press.

Levine, A., & Hirsch, D. (1990, November 7). Student activism and optimism return to campuses. *The Chronicle of Higher Education,* p. A48.

LeVine, R.A. (1966). American college experience as a socialization process. In T.M. Newcomb and E.K. Wilson (Eds.), *College peer groups: Problems and prospects for research* (pp. 107–132). Chicago: Aldine.

Love, P.G. (1990). *An investigation into the organizational culture of a student affairs department.* Unpublished doctoral dissertation. Indiana University, Bloomington, IN.

Moffatt, M. (1988) *Coming of age in New Jersey: College and American culture.* New Brunswick, NJ: Rutgers University Press.

Morgan, G. (1986). *Images of organization.* Beverly Hills, CA: Sage.

Morrill, W.H., Hurst, J.C. and Associates (Eds.) (1980). *Dimensions of intervention for student development.* New York: Wiley.

Newcomb, T.M. (1961). *The acquaintance process.* New York: Holt, Rinehart, and Winston.

Newcomb, T.M. (1962). Student peer-group influence. In N. Sanford (Ed.), *The American college: A psychological and social interpretation of the higher learning* (pp. 469–488). New York: Wiley.

Newcomb, T.M., & Wilson, E.K. (1966). *College peer groups: Problems and prospects for research.* Chicago: Aldine.

Newcomb, T.M., Koenig, K.E., Flacks, R. & Warwick, D.P. (1967). *Persistence and change: Bennington College and its students after twenty–five years.* New York: Wiley.

Pace, C.R., & Baird, L.L. (1966). Attainment patterns in the environmental press of college subcultures. In T.M. Newcomb & E.K. Wilson (Eds.), *College peer groups: Problems and prospects for research* (pp. 215–242). Chicago: Aldine.

Pascarella, E.T., & Terenzini, P.T. (1991). *How college affects students*. San Francisco: Jossey-Bass.

Schlossberg, N.K. (1989). Marginality and mattering: Key issues in building community. In D. Roberts (Ed.), *Designing campus activities to foster a sense of community, New Directions for Student Services*, No. 48 (pp. 5–13). San Francisco, CA: Jossey-Bass.

Schlossberg, N.K., Lynch, A.Q., & Chickering, A.W. (1989). *Improving higher education environments for adults: Responsive programs and services from entry to departure*. San Francisco: Jossey-Bass.

Sergiovanni, T.J. (1984). Cultural and competing perspectives in administrative theory and practice. In T.J. Sergiovanni and J.E. Corbally (Eds.), *Leadership and organizational culture* (pp. 1–11). Urbana, IL: University of Illinois Press.

Tierney, W. (1987). The symbolic aspects of leadership: An ethnographic perspective. *The American Journal of Semiotics, 5*, 233–50.

Tinto, V. (1987). *Leaving college: Rethinking the causes and cures of student attrition*. Chicago: University of Chicago Press.

Upcraft, M.L., & Pilato, G.T. (1982). *Residence hall assistants in college: A guide to selection, training, and supervision*. San Francisco: Jossey-Bass.

Van Maanen, J. (1987, May). *Managing education better: Some thoughts on the management of student cultures in American colleges and universities*. Paper presented at the annual meeting of the Association for Institutional Research, Kansas City, Mo.

Weidman, J.C. (1989). Undergraduate socialization: A conceptual approach. In J.C. Smart (Ed.), *Higher education: Handbook for theory and research*, Vol. 5 (pp. 289–322). New York: Agathon.

CHAPTER 5

"Making the
Familiar Strange":
Discovering Culture

Elizabeth J. Whitt

INTRODUCTION

Asked for his advice on acting, Spencer Tracy once remarked, "Just
know your lines and don't bump into the furniture." On the stage of
organizational culture, such advice becomes wholly inadequate.
Actors within collegiate cultures have few if any scripts to go by.
And as for the furniture, the most visible props are not the ones we
tend to bump into. Rather we most often trip over perceptions and
attitudes, the intangibles that escape our attention even as they make
up the fabric of daily organizational life (Chaffee & Tierney, 1988,
p. 3).

Culture and its influences on behaviors in organizations are not
readily apparent. Members of a subculture or subgroup, such as a
student affairs division, have difficulty identifying aspects of their
own culture because these elements have become second nature.
People accept as commonplace the cultural properties that shape
their behavior. For example, the influence of a beloved dean—a
departmental hero or heroine—on how staff view their jobs and
students may be taken for granted until that person decides to re-
tire. In this chapter, methods of discovering institutional cultures
are described. Emphasis is given to the use of qualitative inquiry
methods for identifying aspects of culture and understanding how
culture influences behavior.

DISCOVERING CULTURE

The picture that we have painted of the culture of a student affairs organization is complicated: layers, levels, and elements of
culture coming together to form an invisible tapestry (Kuh & Whitt,
1988)—a tapestry in that all of the bits and pieces make a picture
that is more beautiful and interesting than each of the components,
invisible in that it tends to exist below the level of consciousness
of organizational participants.

If that is the case—if an institution's culture is, in fact, invisible
to insiders—how can it be discovered by someone (insider or outsider) who would like to try to identify and understand its nature?
Obviously, such discovery is something that cannot be done quickly,
but it *can* be done if the investigator is willing to keep an open
mind while wearing the cultural lenses (concepts, framework, appreciation) we have provided.

Two possible approaches to discovering the culture, or cultures,
of an institution are: (a) making the familiar strange by viewing
one's own organization from the perspective of an outsider (Morgan, 1989), and (b) a culture audit, a systematic process of discovery that can be conducted by insiders and outsiders both working
in cooperation. These approaches can be used separately or together,
depending on the desired type and level of understanding and the
amount of time and effort available.

MAKING THE FAMILIAR STRANGE

In order to gain new insights into the culture of your own organization, it can be helpful to approach it from the perspective of a
visitor to a foreign country (Morgan, 1989). For example, consider
the following questions: When you were a newcomer to the organization, what was unexpected or strange about the way things were
done, how people behaved, the language people used, or the assumptions that people made? If you wanted to describe to an outsider the essential nature of your organization, what stories would
you tell, and why? What should a visitor see and to whom should
a visitor speak if she wanted to understand your organization?

Newcomers are sometimes mystified by such student affairs "jar-
gon" as—"milieu management", "student development", "Kohl-
berg's levels", and the like—language that, depending on its institutional context, may reflect a deep commitment to the use of
theoretical frameworks to understand students' growth, or training
in a single graduate program, or the need to reinforce student af-

fairs staff identity. Over time, the newcomer learns the meanings behind the words and no longer feels like an outsider (Whitt, 1990).

Thinking about, or talking as a group about, an organization from an outsider's perspective can reveal the practices and underlying values and assumptions which are often taken for granted, thereby bringing cultural elements to a level of consciousness so they can be examined and understood. In addition, taking an outsider's view may illuminate elements of the culture that need to be challenged. For example, does the language used by student affairs staff isolate them from other parts of the institution, or even from the students they are committed to serve? What values are reflected in the stories told about the student affairs organization? Are those the values student affairs staff purport to hold? What is expressed about your culture by the places and people you think a visitor must see in order to understand your organization? Perhaps you would show the student affairs office where staff members are separated from one another and from students by walls, partitions, and secretaries desks; perhaps this arrangement illustrates a lack of communication and shared values among student affairs staff. The intent of taking an outsider's perspective is not, of course, to focus only on problems, but to provide fresh insights into the culture.

THE CULTURE AUDIT

The culture audit provides both insiders and outsiders with a means to systematically discover and identify the artifacts, values, and assumptions that comprise an organization's culture (Fetterman, 1987; Kuh & Whitt, 1988). Use of the word "systematic" implies that culture is not something that one can simply go looking for, nor should it be found in everything everyone says or does. In the following sections, the uses of culture audits, guiding principles and techniques for performing an audit, and a sample culture audit are described.

Uses of the Culture Audit

A culture audit gives the investigator a map to use in exploring the culture of an institution or some smaller entity, such as a division of student affairs or a residence hall. Culture audits also allow for many useful "side trips" from the planned journey. Thus, a culture audit is a flexible framework for the process of discovery. For example, an effective audit design will ensure that the investigator seeks and finds many and varied perspectives—multiple insider views—about the culture (Kuh & Whitt, 1988), but does not attempt to define all sources of those perspectives in advance.

Once completed, an effective culture audit enables the investigator to describe the culture in ways that are useful to and appreciated by both insiders and outsiders (Whitt & Kuh, 1991). Insiders will recognize the culture portrayed by the investigator as their own, but will find new insights as well. Outsiders will, to the extent possible, obtain a "native's" view of the culture, including insider meanings and understandings about the less visible aspects of culture.

Guiding Principles for Performing a Culture Audit

There are eight guiding principles to keep in mind before embarking on the exploration of an institution's culture, whether your own or another.

Principle 1: Take heed of Masland's (1985) assertion that "(c)ulture is implicit and we are all embedded in our own cultures" (p. 160). Therefore, before undertaking a culture audit, Auditors must identify and acknowledge their assumptions about culture in general, such as the elements culture encompasses, its usefulness as a lens for understanding organizations, and how visible or invisible the culture is likely to be. Auditors' assumptions about the culture of the organization to be studied should also be considered. Auditors must be willing to suspend judgment about what will or will not be found in the process of the audit, a task that may be especially difficult for inside auditors. Insiders may be so familiar with the organization that they fail to notice important, yet tacit, aspects of the culture, or let their assumptions about the culture influence what is seen and how it is interpreted (Crowson, 1987).

Principle 2: Respect the uniqueness and integrity of the institution or division you are studying: "learn its identity in the same way [you] learn to know a valued friend" (Chaffee & Tierney, 1988, p. 4). Avoid generalizing from other experiences or organizations or placing a veil of "shoulds" or "should nots" over what you see. Do not, for example, make evaluative judgments about the worth of a particular practice, symbol, story, or hero; instead, find out what it means to people within the culture and how it influences their attitudes and behavior.

Principle 3: Recognize that a rich and relevant picture of a culture requires joint exploration on the part of both outsiders and insiders (Kuh et al, 1991; Schein, 1985). Thus, inside auditors should the seek the assistance of at least one outsider. Outside auditors should find one or more insiders with whom to discuss the emerging cultural picture. Because the process of discovering culture is iterative—involving repeated cycles of data collection and analysis—auditors must continually check their perceptions with the sources of those perceptions. The issue of debriefing with insiders and outsiders will be discussed in more detail later in the chapter.

Principle 4: The discovery of an institution's culture demands lengthy engagement with that culture, or as lengthy an engagement as is possible (Lincoln & Guba, 1985; Schein, 1985). In determining how much time will be needed, consideration must be given to three issues: (a) available resources, such as time, the number of auditors, and money; (b) the focus of the audit: an entire institution, a student affairs division, a residence hall; and (c) the size and complexity of the institution, division, or department to be audited. In a recent study of students' out-of-class experiences, teams of three and four investigators spent six to eight days on each of 14 campuses over the course of two semesters; this was the minimum determined to be useful in obtaining a rich and accurate picture of the issues under investigation (Whitt & Kuh, 1991).

Principle 5: Relevant to time of engagement is the fifth principle: "complicate yourself" (Weick, 1979). Resist the impulse to simplify what you see by focusing on interviews with department heads or persons whose attitudes you share, or moving quickly to draw conclusions about the culture you are studying. Instead, try to get as much and as diverse information as you can by looking for contradictions and differences of opinion (Lincoln & Guba, 1985; Whitt, 1991).

Principle 6: Acknowledge and respect the fact that the institution or organization may not be ready or willing to accept exploration of or feedback about its culture (Schein, 1985). Do not undertake a culture audit without the permission of the participants; do not interview anyone without being very clear about your purposes and the ways in which the information obtained from them will be used (Lincoln & Guba, 1985). Avoid reporting preliminary findings except as necessary for checking your emerging constructions (that is your impressions, explanations, and interpretations) with insiders; until insiders have confirmed your constructions of their culture, you have no findings. Also, consider carefully any request to share the outcomes of your exploration with persons who may be interested in using your constructions for their own purposes. Be very explicit about the ways the results of your study should and should not be used. For example, can the results be used as a basis for policy making? As a rationale for loss of funding? As a press release promoting the institution? A culture audit requires attention to the ethics of research (cf, Goetz & LeCompte, 1984; Lincoln & Guba, 1985) and sensitivity to the people, politics, needs, agendas, norms, expectations, and values—the *culture*—of the institution or organization being studied.

Principle 7: Schein (1985) has stated that, in attempting to discover the culture of an organization, "the only safe approach is triangulation" (p. 135). Multiple data collection techniques, such as interviews and observations, and multiple sources of information, including students and faculty, should be used to get as complex and accurate a picture as possible (Whitt, 1991).

Principle 8: Auditors should seek insiders' perspectives about the understandings and impressions that emerge during the processes of data collection and analysis (Kuh et al., 1991). Continuous feedback from persons within the culture about the auditors' emerging interpretations is essential to help auditors create a picture of the culture that accurately reflects the experiences of insiders.

With these principles and the complex approach to discovering culture they demand in mind, you can begin the process of a culture audit. In the following sections, that process is described in detail.

Methods for Discovery

The inquiry methods recommended for a culture audit are qualitative, producing data in the form of words and analyzing data by means of a "human instrument"—the auditors themselves (Lincoln & Guba, 1985). Qualitative research methods are particularly useful in identifying and understanding the nature of culture and cultural processes (Goetz & LeCompte, 1984; Morgan, 1986). Values, beliefs, and assumptions are complicated constructs that are most accessible to investigation by interviews and observation and analysis of verbal data (Goetz & LeCompte, 1984; Whitt, 1991).

Data collection. Particularly useful techniques for collecting data during a culture audit include interviews, document analysis, and observation. Documents, including handbooks, policy manuals, catalogues, and institutional histories are reviewed before and during the site visit in order to obtain information and gain impressions about the organization and its context, and to generate interview questions (Dobbert, 1984). As the audit progresses, auditors will become aware of other documents that can be used to fill in gaps in knowledge about the culture and to develop further interview questions (Whitt & Kuh, 1991).

Interviews should be conducted in a variety of formats, such as focus groups and individual interviews, to elicit as many perspectives about the culture from as many people as possible. Focus groups (Merton, Fisk, & Kendall, 1956; MacMillin, 1989) are discussion groups that meet only once for a specific purpose, such as talking about the values extant in a student affairs organization or the assumptions underlying an institution's mission. Some members of the organization, such as the founding president, graduating seniors, and the institutional historian, may be particularly rich sources of cultural information, and so individual interviews would be appropriate to obtain their unique perspectives (Whitt & Kuh, 1991).

An initial set of questions should be developed to provide direction for the interviews, although the interviews should not be so structured that fruitful areas of information about which you are unaware are missed. If, for example, you plan to talk with students only about their out-of-class experiences, you may miss important information about the quality of their lives in the institution. Plan on being fairly flexible at the start of the audit—when you do not yet know all of what you do not know (Lincoln & Guba, 1985)—and more structured as your findings and interpretations develop and the gaps in your knowledge are more apparent (Whitt, 1991). You may discover that the physical environment of the institution has a much more significant impact on student life than you had anticipated, and so may want to talk with the institution's architect and physical plant personnel.

Observations of events, activities, and programs can be a useful source of information about the culture as well as a source of additional interview questions (Whitt, 1991). Some activities or times of the year, such as commencement, homecoming, and the beginning of the fall semester, may hold more promise for cultural exploration than others. At such times, the history and values of the institution are vividly portrayed in ceremonies, traditions, and speeches.

Do not, however, miss the potentially useful cultural information that can be gathered from seemingly mundane activities (Morgan, 1986) such as staff meetings, passing between classes, and meal times. If auditors focus only on events which are most colorful or most obvious, the daily routines that give life to institutional values and assumptions will be missed (Kuh et al, 1991). Homecoming may be the *only* time that community members gather to celebrate. Statements made by students, faculty, and administrators during new student orientation and opening convocation about the importance of rigorous academic effort may be contradicted in the daily lives of students. Institutional leaders may make impressive speeches about the college's commitment to becoming a pluralistic learning community, while women and people of color may be treated as invisible in staff meetings, committee assignments, and the student press.

Sources of Information

People. People are likely to be your primary source of information about the culture you are studying. When deciding whom to interview, keep in mind the need to discover as many different perspectives as possible so that you may obtain as accurate a picture of the culture as possible.

Sampling techniques appropriate to a culture audit include status and snowball sampling (Dobbert, 1984). Status sampling is the selection of respondents according to their role in the organization, such as dean, department head, student. In your effort to gather multiple perspectives regarding the culture, you should interview from as broad a spectrum of roles as possible (Dobbert, 1984; Whitt, 1991). For example, if studying a student affairs organization, administrators from all levels, junior and senior faculty, students (on-campus and off-campus, all class levels, white and people of color, women and men) alumnae/i, board members, and other constituents should be included.

The process of snowball sampling expands the native views avail-

able for the audit (Dobbert, 1984). At the end of each interview
with persons obtained by status sampling, ask them to identify others with whom you should talk in order to better understand the
culture, or ask them to identify persons whose views are different
from their own. Snowball sampling will help you obtain more varied understandings and interpretations of the institution or organization and, it is hoped, a more complex and accurate picture of the
culture (Whitt, 1991).

Documents. Useful sources of written information about a culture include student newspapers, admissions publications, development publications, planning documents, policies and procedures
manuals, job descriptions, budgets, student/faculty/staff handbooks,
and catalogues; each of these represents ways in which the institution describes itself to others or implements (or fails to implement)
its values. Any or all of these documents should be studied prior to
talking with members of the culture (or prior to entering the organization) to obtain an outsider's view of the culture as well as to
help develop interview questions (Whitt & Kuh, 1991). Additional
important documents will, of course, come to your attention during
the interview process, and they should be obtained as needed.

Events and activities. Fruitful sources of information about a
culture range from the day-to-day, such as coffee breaks, faculty
or staff meetings, advising sessions, and residence hall programs,
to the special, such as Fall Convocation, to the spontaneous, such
as demonstrations and protests. At the beginning of an audit, you
can ask for schedules and calendars to help you plan for the events
you need to attend, although you will discover some after the audit
is in progress.

Settings. Opportunities to learn about an organization's culture
may be found anywhere that members of the culture come in contact with one another. Potentially informative settings include residence hall floors, lounges, and lobbies; classrooms and the hallways and stairwells of classroom buildings; offices and reception
areas; student unions and other gathering places; cafeterias; side-
walks; and recreational facilities (Whitt & Kuh, 1991). In any or
all of these settings, auditors play the role of observer to discover
how people in the culture interact with one another in informal
circumstances. Do people greet each other as they pass on the sidewalk? Are there places where community members can come to-

gether without much effort? Do faculty and students continue class-room discussions into hallways or cafeterias? Are residence hall lounges used by residents? Do students of different races sit to-gether at meal times? Do students sit with the same group of people at every meal? Are public areas used to communicate important information about the institution? If auditors decide to approach people to ask them about their activities or their experiences, the potential respondents should be informed of the purpose of the conversation and should give consent before being interviewed (Lincoln & Guba, 1985).

A Sample Culture Audit

The following sample culture audit (Kuh et al, in press; Kuh & Whitt, 1988; Schein, 1985) is offered as an example of the culture audit process. The steps to be taken, however, must be tailored to fit the needs of the auditors, the institutional culture to be audited, and the purpose and focus of the audit.

Phase One: Advance Preparation. Prior to beginning the audit:

1. Schedule the visit through a contact person. Decide whom to interview (status sampling) and arrange as many interviews in ad-vance as possible. Decisions about information to be discovered, whom to interview, questions to ask, and so forth, should be deter-mined by the specific purposes of the audit and the institutional context. Emphasize to the contact person the necessity of obtain-ing many and diverse views of the institution. Also, make arrange-ments for interview rooms (for focus groups and individuals) and workspace for the auditors (for team meetings, document storage, personal belongings).

2. Send letters to persons who will be interviewed (respondents) explaining the purpose of the visit and the types of information you are seeking. The letters should be written, and signed, by the auditors (or the lead auditor), but the institutional contact person should be sure that they are delivered to the respondents before the interviews.

3. Develop summary forms for recording data, including an-swers to interview questions, developing themes and interpretations, and generating further interview questions. Such forms will enable collection of similar information across auditors and data sources and provide a convenient means to keep a record of data collected,

from whom, by whom, and when. Useful forms include interview summary forms, document summary forms, and observation summary forms (Miles & Huberman, 1984; Whitt & Kuh, 1991).

4. Obtain documents likely to provide insights into the culture, as well as to facilitate formulation of interview questions. Again, the institutional contact person can be helpful in gathering documents. Study the documents and make notes of the messages they convey about the culture on the document summary forms.

5. Develop interview protocols for each set of respondents. Initial questions should be developed from the focus of the audit as well as information gleaned from institutional contact persons, document analysis, and literature regarding institutional culture (cf, Chaffee & Tierney, 1988; Kuh & Whitt, 1988). Keep in mind that new questions will emerge as the study progresses.

6. Develop consent forms to be signed by all respondents. Make sure that the forms meet institutional requirements for research with human subjects. Useful information for consent forms includes a statement of the purpose of the audit, a description of the responsibilities of the auditors, such as confidentiality and obtaining permission to quote respondents, and the rights of the respondents, such as to withdraw from the audit at any time.

Phase Two: Entry.

1. Obtain written permission from respondents to talk with them.

2. By means of interviews (with groups and individuals), observations, and further document analysis:
   a. identify, examine, and describe cultural artifacts, such as institutional history and traditions, policies and practices, language, and values (artifacts are discussed in Chapters One and Two);
   b. find divergent viewpoints, such as through snowball sampling;
   c. look for contradictions and surprises.

3a. For audit teams: Meet each day after interviews are completed to discuss your experiences. These meetings should be used to generate questions for future interviews, identify additional respondents who should be interviewed and additional events that should be observed, and begin to identify patterns and themes in the data collected.

3b. For single auditors: If you are an outsider to the culture, locate an insider who is willing to help you in your exploration and who is capable of providing assistance in discovering the organization's culture. If you are an insider, locate an outsider who is willing and able to serve as a "sounding board." After your first round of interviews and observations, reveal to this person your impressions and questions about the culture, including the surprises and contradictions. Work together to probe for the basic assumptions underlying the artifacts and surprises. Identify working "hunches" or explanations.

4. After the first round of interviews, hold debriefing sessions with groups of respondents and additional members of the culture to get their feedback on the auditors' interpretations and understandings of the data collected to this point. Time spent in debriefing will be most effective if the respondents receive a written report of the auditors' "findings" in advance of the meeting.

5. Conduct further interviews, observations, and document analyses. At this point, you know more about what you do not know, what you need to find out, and additional sources of information. The process of "filling in the gaps" may require one or more additional visits to the institution.

6. Conduct further debriefings with respondents. The debriefing process should continue along with data collection and analysis.

Phase Three: Tentative Constructions.

1. Develop, in writing, a tentative report of your discoveries, impressions, explanations, and descriptions of artifacts, values, and assumptions.

2. Provide copies of your report to your respondents and your institutional contact person. Ask each person to read and react to the report, providing elaborations and/or corrections for your interpretations. If possible, present your report and get respondents' feedback in person.

Phase Four: Exit.

1. Seek additional information as needed on the basis of reactions to the first report.

2. Make additions and corrections to the report.

3. Once again, obtain feedback from respondents and institu-

tional contacts about your constructions and conclusions. Continue this process until the members of the culture feel that you have accurately reflected their views of the culture. If there is disagreement among persons within the culture about the auditors' interpretations, work to understand the differences and why disagreement exists. The absence of a shared view of the culture can be an important finding of the audit.

If auditors find themselves in disagreement with the feedback, they should make sure that there is solid evidence of their interpretations in the data (from all data sources and from previous debriefings). Remember, however, that the auditors' report should portray the perceptions and perspectives of the persons within the culture; work with them to negotiate a final product with which both auditors and respondents can agree.

4. Provide a final report to the institution or organization.

5. Thank all of the respondents and contact persons, in writing, for their assistance.

SUMMARY

Discovering the culture of an organization or institution is a complex task that requires much time, effort, and willingness to suspend judgment. Whether you choose to look at your own organization from the perspective of an outsider or undertake a culture audit, the potential reward is greater understanding of both the visible and the tacit elements—the furniture, scripts, and invisible props—that constitute institutional culture.

REFERENCES

Chaffee, E.E., and Tierney, W.G. (1988). *Collegiate culture and leadership strategies.* New York: American Council on Education/Macmillan.

Dobbert, M.L. (1984). *Ethnographic research: Theory and application for modern schools and societies.* New York: Prager.

Fetterman, D. (1987). *Ethnographic auditing: A new approach to evaluating management in higher education.* Paper presented at the Annual Meeting of the American Educational Research Association, Washington, D.C.

Goetz, J.P., & LeCompte, M.D. (1984). *Ethnography and qualitative design in educational research.* Orlando, FL: Academic Press.

Kuh, G.D., Schuh, J.H., Whitt, E.J., Andreas, R.E., Lyons, J.W., Strange, C.C., Krehbiel, L.E., & MacKay, K.A. (1991). *Involving colleges: Successful approaches to fostering student learning and personal development outside the classroom* . San Francisco: Jossey–Bass.

Kuh, G.D., & Whitt, E.J. (1988). *The invisible tapestry: Cultures in American colleges and universities.* ASHE-ERIC Higher Education Report, No. 1. Washington, DC: Association for the Study of Higher Education.

Lincoln, Y.S., & Guba, E.G. (1985). *Naturalistic inquiry.* Beverly Hills, CA: Sage.

McMillin, J.H. (1989). *Focus group interviews: Implications for educational research.* Paper presented at the Annual Meeting of the American Educational Research Association, San Francisco.

Merton, R.K., Fisk, M., & Kendall, P.L. (1956). *The focused interview.* New York: Free Press.

Miles, M.B., & Huberman, A.M. (1984). *Qualitative data analysis: A sourcebook of new methods.* Beverly Hills, CA: Sage.

Morgan, G. (1986). *Images of organization.* Beverly Hills, CA: Sage.

Morgan, G. (1989). *Creative organization theory: A sourcebook.* Newbury Park, CA: Sage.

Schein, E.H. (1985). *Organizational culture and leadership.* San Francisco: Jossey-Bass.

Weick, K.E. (1979). *The social psychology of organizing.* Reading, MA: Addison-Wesley.

Whitt, E.J. (Spring, 1990). "Don't drink the water?": A guide to encountering a new institutional culture. *Connections: A publication for new professionals in student affairs*, 2–10.

Whitt, E.J. (1991). Artful science: A primer on qualitative research methods. *Journal of College Student Development, 32,* 406–415.

Whitt, E.J., & Kuh, G.D. (1991). The use of qualitative methods in a team approach to multiple institution studies. *The Review of Higher Education, 14,* 317–337.

CHAPTER 6

Loosening the Ties That Bind: Shaping Student Culture

Kathleen Manning
Shevawn Bogdan Eaton

As is clear from the preceding chapters, campus culture has long been a topic of interest and study (Bushnell, 1962; Clark, 1970; Horowitz, 1987; Kuh & Whitt, 1988; Manning, 1989; Sanford, 1962). Culture has been defined variously, such as "the social or normative glue that holds an organization together" (Siehl, 1985, p. 125) or "a process of reality construction that allows people to see and understand particular events, actions, objects, utterances, or situations in distinctive ways" (Morgan, 1986, p. 128). Similar to institutional culture, student culture is composed of the normative behavior and shared values, meanings, and beliefs of students (Chapter 4, Kuh & Whitt, 1988). Student culture shapes, encourages, and rewards certain behaviors over others, even though some behaviors may be in conflict with the institution's values.

One aspect of campus culture that eludes consensus is whether culture, specifically student culture, can be managed, changed, or shaped.

> Those researchers who argue that culture is a socially constructed system of shared beliefs and values would find it inconsistent to think of systematically managing or attempting to control the phenomenon. . . . However, other researchers . . . would seem to hold a hope . . . that culture can be managed, at least to some degree (Siehl, 1985, p. 125).

William Bennett (1984) and Ernest Boyer (1987) have challenged student affairs professionals to shape student culture in ways that emphasize, rather than ignore, institutional standards of academic and social achievement. Although the type of intentional, predictable modification of student culture suggested by Bennett and Boyer is difficult to produce (Kuh & Whitt, 1988), there are strategies that support desired changes in student culture. Indeed, if one believes that social reality is constantly being created and recreated through human action (Lewis, 1980; Marcus, 1988), culture can be influenced, although not in predictable ways. "The question should be changed from, 'Can culture be managed?' to `when and what aspects of culture can be managed'" (Siehl, 1985, p. 126).

This chapter examines interventions designed to purposefully influence student culture in a manner that encourages student learning and personal development consistent with an institution's educational purposes. These suggestions are offered with the full acknowledgement of the accidents, unavoidable circumstances, and expressions of Murphy's law (i.e., "whatever can go wrong, will go wrong") which are inherent in culture-shaping efforts put forth by student affairs professionals in working with students, faculty, and other administrators.

WHO IS RESPONSIBLE
FOR STUDENT CULTURE?

When trying to shape aspects of student culture, numerous questions surface that demand consideration. Can student affairs professionals promote change in student culture consistent with their institution's educational purposes? Can professional staff use current debates about multiculturalism in constructive ways in their attempts at cultural change? How can multicultural perspectives be introduced successfully into the dominant student culture?

The perpetuation of student traditions that alienate certain groups of students and work against attaining institutional goals is an ongoing subject of concern for student affairs professionals. Many traditions perpetuated by the student culture (e.g., initiation rites) have excluded or—at the least—not acknowledged the backgrounds of some historically underrepresented groups (e.g., Christmas tree lighting ceremonies, Kuh & MacKay, 1989). Fraternities and sororities, in particular, have been criticized for sustaining traditions out of step with the needs of today's campuses (Horowitz, 1987; Kuh & Lyons, 1990; Maisel, 1990). As discussed in Chapter 2, compounding the concern about exclusion are institutional messages embedded in cultural artifacts which are both positive *and* negative (e.g., racism *and* community, fraternity *and* exclusion). Leadership training programs rarely acknowledge the skills of adult learners or encourage their participation (Sartorelli & Fisher, 1992). Student development theory does not adequately account for the development of students of color (McEwen, Roper, Bryant, & Langa, 1990). As a result, some of what have become traditional practices in student affairs programming are paradoxical; that is, they engender positive feelings (e.g., affiliation) in some people and negative feelings (e.g., isolation) in others.

As mentioned in Chapter 2, it is rare that the values and assumptions underlying cultural artifacts are exclusively negative and, therefore, easy to eliminate. Nor are their messages uniformly positive, and, therefore, worthy of support. Instead, the multiple messages associated with cultural artifacts are often interpreted differently by various groups; thus, it is not surprising that some are openly debated. The results of this debate may be both edifying and divisive. The following section describes a model for cultural change that uses transitions endemic to college and university life (Kanter, 1983; Siehl, 1985) as opportunities to examine some of the underlying values and assumptions of an institution's student cultures (Astin, 1985; Horowitz, 1987; Moffatt, 1989).

A MODEL FOR SHAPING STUDENT CULTURE

Recall from the preceding chapters that culture is tenacious. The undergirding assumptions of student culture persist through generations of students despite change efforts on the part of administrators and faculty. The reader is advised to bear in mind this caveat when considering the process model which follows.

Triggers for Change

Siehl (1985) found that certain transitions often serve as triggers for cultural change. These transition situations, externally or internally induced, can be used as opportunities to influence values expressed in the student culture. The challenge to student affairs staff, then, is to capitalize on impending transitions in order to gain an educational advantage for the institution and its students.

Environmental calamities. Environmental calamities are crises or phenomena which *cannot* be ignored by a healthy institution (Siehl, 1985). Calamities include sharp decreases in institutional funds (e.g., state-mandated rescissions), demographic shifts (e.g., increase in part-time students or students of color), changes in state law (e.g., change in drinking age), and other outside influences which have effects on the characteristics of students and their attitudes and behavior. Environmental calamities produce cultural change whether or not the organization is prepared for such effects.

Many colleges anticipated the end of the "baby boom" as an impending environmental calamity. Because of declining numbers of traditional-aged students, colleges modified their recruitment methods and admissions criteria to attract older students (many of whom were commuters and enrolled part-time), established continuing education departments as an alternative source of income, and developed initiatives to improve retention rates of certain groups, such as Latino and African American students, because the number of students from these groups were predicted to increase rather than decrease (Hodgkinson, 1984).

Environmental opportunities. This category includes such environmental triggers as the development of satellite technology and the introduction of new majors to respond to student demand. At some institutions, adding majors such as computer science or engineering resulted in an influx of students with different values than those of earlier cohorts of students. In some instances, this also increased the number of students who had values compatible with those of the faculty (e.g., firm commitment to the academic quality), a turn of events which can energize faculty and ratchet upward expectations for academic achievement for the entire student body.

While demographic shifts can be calamities, colleges also can turn changing characteristics of students into opportunities. Decreasing birth rates of white students coupled with increasing enrollments of African Americans and Latinos in some areas of the country (Hodgkinson, 1984) have influenced the student cultures at many colleges as the complexion of student bodies changed literally from mostly white to multicolored. Over time, the changes, of course, will become deeper and more profound than skin color as a variety of cultures (e.g., rural, urban, in-state, out-of-state, gay and lesbian, women) come together. Creating a sense of community on campus out of these diverse groups while celebrating differences and maintaining respect for their unique characteristics is an environmental challenge that must be turned into an educational opportunity.

Internal revolutions. The third category of triggers are revolutions that arise from within the institution. Internal revolutions may be stimulated by hiring new staff (e.g., president) or by student-initiated issues. For example, a new president may use the "honeymoon" period to introduce and test reactions to different values, policies, and priorities. Campus protests by students of color during the 1980s and 1990s frequently used such militant actions as building takeovers, interruption of governing board meetings, and disruption of classes. These actions can be considered internal revolutions, particularly if they stimulate changes in organizational structures, policies, and practices. Themes across these protests included calls to stamp out institutionalized racism, efforts to implement ethnic studies majors and a multicultural curriculum, and initiatives to attract and retain more students and faculty of color (Altbach & Lomotey, 1991).

The triggers and transitions described above result in planned and unplanned cultural changes. Of course, in the best of all possible worlds, cultural change should not be left to chance but, rather, purposefully and carefully planned (Kanter, 1983). Changes should be orchestrated in such a way so that, as a result of the change, students' values and assumptions more closely mirror the educational ideals for which their institution stands.

> What imbues this [cultural change] with meaning . . . is not just the sense of being part of a group, but the *significance* of the tasks taken on: the feeling of pride and accomplishment at building—and building something relevant (Kanter, 1983, p. 203).

Steps Toward Cultural Change

In this section, a five-step process model is outlined to effect desirable changes in student culture.

1. Identify values and assumptions (Siehl, 1985). Any attempt to shape culture must begin with an examination of the values and assumptions that undergird student culture. Values "reflect the espoused as well as the enacted ideals of an institution or group" (Chapter 1). Examples of values embedded within student culture are reflected in expectations for academic achievement, beliefs about human differences, and aspirations for personal and collective actions, all of which are influenced by students' backgrounds and previous experiences (Van Maanen, 1984).

Assumptions are the "tacit beliefs that members use to define their role, their relationships to others, and the nature of the organization in which they live" (Chapter 1). As such, they are the taken-for-granted beliefs upon which students act. Recall that because assumptions are tacit, they are harder to discover than values because people rarely express them orally or in writing. Examples of this level of student culture include students' struggles to put into words their feelings about faith, their expectations of relationships with others, and principles upon which they live their lives.

Examination of yearbooks, student newspapers, and other student-generated documents may reveal some guiding values and assumptions. Similarly, some values and assumptions of student culture can be discovered by examining the language students use. The more subtle aspects of student culture, however, can only be understood with student cooperation and assistance. Because students are the only source of expert testimony, communication between students and administrators is key. As described in Chapter 5, administrators and students involved in the cultural change process need to listen so that they "see" and "hear" cultural aspects generally hidden from view. Both students and administrators must strive for "remarkable openmindedness . . . willingness to listen, nondefensiveness, and ability to let go of an investment in their own ideas in order to pick up on a different idea" (Kanter, 1983, p. 136).

2. Assess level of commitment to values and assumptions (Siehl, 1985). The second step in shaping student culture is to assess the level of commitment of various student groups to their group's values. Students of color, adult learners, women, and gay and lesbian students may adhere to a set of cultural values and assumptions different from that expressed on campus by members of fraternities. Students disenfranchised from the dominant student culture may feel isolated by the lack of opportunities to express and act on their beliefs. The task for student affairs administrators is to identify the diverse values and assumptions which have not been historically assimilated into the larger student culture and attempt to create opportunities for members of disenfranchised groups to participate in as many aspects of campus life as possible. Thus, in addition to the communication mentioned in the first step, students should be encouraged, and given permission, to honestly communicate their culture's values and assumptions, the focus of the next step.

3. *Create opportunities for wider expression of alternative values.* Student advisory committees are one vehicle for obtaining input from and initiating collaboration with students. It is important that participants represent a diverse range of opinions and perspectives. The deliberate inclusion of adult students, students of color, women, commuters, and international students on student advisory committees, for example, is a step toward insuring that diverse perspectives and values are represented in institutional governance. When people from different backgrounds come together, conflict is not unusual. In order to create an atmosphere in which the expression of divergent opinions is valued, conflict cannot be avoided nor should it be prematurely suppressed. Rather, the goal of such advisory committee work is not to produce consensus of opinion, but to solicit multiple perspectives that accurately represent various points of view. Thus, management of such committees requires that the student affairs professional possess effective negotiation and mediation skills.

4. *Introduce cultural interventions.* The fourth step is to design interventions including face-to-face communication, role modeling, and the introduction of cultural artifacts that symbolize desired behavior and institutional values (Siehl, 1985). Cultural interventions are more likely to succeed when they are initiated as part of the anticipatory socialization of new students (Van Maanen, 1984). For example, a university in the southwest has emphasized the importance of public service by selectively recruiting upperclass students who share this interest and matching them with new students during summer orientation and again during fall orientation. Administrators and student paraprofessionals talk a lot with new students about the importance of service and about the institution's tradition of providing service to the local community and beyond.

In this case, the cultural intervention was designed to reinforce institutional values. In other cases, however, interventions may challenge certain values and assumptions of the student culture that are antithetical to the institution's mission and philosophy. With careful analysis, cultural artifacts, communication, and role modeling can re-shape student culture to a form that reflects the increasing diversity of perspectives inherent in the contemporary campus culture.

5. Assess behavior changes (Siehl, 1985). As a direct expression of cultural values and assumptions, student behavior reflects values and assumptions. Thus, the final step of the cultural change model is to determine whether intended behavior changes resulted from the cultural intervention. This step, similar to program and policy evaluation, assesses whether the tactics used to address culture actually achieved the desired change.

CULTURAL INTERVENTIONS

Any strategy used to shape student cultures can be interpreted in the framework of the change model outlined above. In this section, examples are offered of how symbols, language, policies and practices, and student leadership styles can be used individually, or in various combinations, to influence student culture.

Symbols

Students, faculty, and administrators live within a cultural framework bounded by certain themes: academic freedom, collegial governance, professional autonomy. These themes are reflected in symbols which serve as vehicles for meaning (Ortner, 1984) and often represent complex ideologies (Turner, 1977a). Symbols "carry implicit messages. . . . When they are well chosen and understood, they do their work unnoticed" (Myerhoff, 1984, p. 160). For example, ivy covered buildings represent high academic aspirations and legitimate certain behaviors (e.g., contemplation and reflection). Academic regalia worn by faculty and students during commencement and convocations is a reminder that the origins of the American higher education system date back to medieval Europe.

Symbols, by definition, are multivocal (Turner, 1977b). Rather than conveying *only one meaning*, symbols often evoke many interpretations, ideas, and actions. This multivocality can be used to encourage acceptance of different perspectives introduced by students from historically underrepresented groups. Thus, the conviction that *many* types of student culture exist is celebrated, nurtured, and communicated through multivocal symbols. The culturally competent administrator remains open-minded about various interpretations of symbols as well as encourages discussion about the multiple meanings of those symbols.

Change is nurtured by symbolically communicating values through public acts. As mentioned in Chapter 7, the symbolic leader uses symbols to express and evoke commitment to the community's values. Symbols also reflect images of what the institution is, as well as a vision of what it could be (Myerhoff, 1977). For example, a vision of an institution's aspirations is expressed through what community leaders and others do and say during ceremonies and other cultural performances. These acts become woven into an college's institution's culture and serve as consistent reminders of its values. Such public celebrations of institutional values encourage people to embrace cultural change consistent with a vision of high quality living and learning opportunities (Manning, 1989). After exposure to the messages exhibited in symbols, participants return to everyday life with new or renewed commitment to the framework presented to them symbolically (Lewis, 1980).

Symbols can be particularly useful in articulating the inclusive purposes and multiple perspectives of campus life. A commitment to a diverse environment is reinforced both symbolically and practically with the appointment of a person of color. Staff appointments carry multiple meanings about both the appointed person's roles (e.g., models for students) and a representation of the university's mission (e.g., building an inclusive environment). This symbolism can backfire, however, if the appointee is not given responsibility *and* authority commensurate with the role. Without responsibility and authority, students, faculty, and staff will perceive such appointments to be tokenism and respond with predictable and understandable frustration. If campuses are to become authentic multicultural learning communities, symbols representing inclusive and exclusive assumptions must be enacted through policy and practice.

Language

The mission of Mount Holyoke College is to provide a unique higher education opportunity designed for women which empha-

sizes achievement and excellence. The language used during Fall
Convocation communicates the values that support this mission. The
president uses the word "women" to refer to new students. Just out
of high school, many new students are surprised at being called a
"woman"—but the message sticks. The message is, "you are women
of distinction" who will perform at a level of excellence while at
the college as well as afterwards. In this way language acknowledges the perspectives of first-year women students while articulating high expectations for their learning and personal development (Manning, 1989). As such, language is a primary vehicle for
the communication of the institution's mission.

Policies and Practices

Policy making and managing are major functions of student affairs professionals. Both occur in a cultural context. The confluence
of institutional, local, and national policies and laws when imple-
mented on campus results in a complex maze of responsibilities
and legal implications (e.g., drinking ages, right to know laws, li-
ability risks). When policies themselves are viewed as cultural artifacts, their symbolic messages become more obvious and can be
more clearly understood by faculty, students, and administrators.
Thus, policy making is an area rich with opportunities to emphasize community values and, therefore, to shape student culture.

Policies that promote faculty-student collaboration on research
emanate from assumptions about the institution's educational mission. Academic honesty policies and honor codes set forth desired
community standards related to integrity and responsibility. Leadership award ceremonies, holiday decorations, and portraits of heroic figures also reflect community values and assumptions. Such
values can be visibly and materially expressed through the kinds
of events and activities that take place in public spaces (e.g., Christmas trees on the campus green), or figuratively through policy (e.g.,
criteria used to bestow awards). College directories that list faculty home addresses and telephone numbers, admission viewbooks
that feature a diverse group of students and activities, and event
calendars that record the scope and functions of co-curricular space
are all manifestations of institutional values enacted through policy.

As campuses struggle to appropriately represent all students in
administrative policy and practice, decisions about who participates
in various governance structures or activities take on greater sig-

nificance. For example, when student organizations are asked to represent student views in policy making, their advice can mask the fact that their input represents a dominant, traditional point of view. Their input may not provide an administrator with an understanding of the range of perspectives on a diverse campus. Rather than relying on one set of groups for ideas, the student affairs professional must be committed to obtaining diverse, more inclusive points of view. Issues of inclusion and exclusion extend to the practices of who gets invited to what events, who is appointed to influential committees, and how resources are allocated to various groups.

In emphasizing issues related to multiculturalism, student affairs professionals must consider public space as a resource and commodity. For example, policy preferences that determine who can use public space, and the purposes for such use, reflect assumptions about privilege and power. Thus, an institution's commitment to include diverse populations is inextricably intertwined with administrative practices concerning the use of culturally defined space.

Student Leadership Styles

Through formal training, socialization to the field's values (Chapter 3), and professional experience, student affairs administrators typically endorse certain student behaviors over others. For example, student leaders who are assertive and sensitive are valued by many student activities staff members. Conference presentations, journal articles, and leadership manuals reinforce particular leadership styles often at the expense of students who do not or cannot behave in a similar manner. Women, in particular, "have demonstrated that using the command-and-control style of managing others, a style generally associated with men . . . is not the only way to succeed" (Rosner, 1990, p. 119). Student behavior that expresses values of participation and inclusion, shared power and information, and enhanced worth of self and of others is becoming increasingly important (Rosner, 1990). Approaches to leadership and followership characterized by competition, debate, and assertiveness need to be viewed as only *one* way to encourage involvement in campus life. Overemphasizing any one style to the exclusion of others ignores the fact that the preferred style is not universally accepted and practiced by all students.

SUMMARY AND ACTIVITIES

To effectively address such campus issues as racial and ethnic strife, the erosion of a sense of community, unclear educational purposes, and student disenchantment with campus life, cultural interventions are needed.

> To manage . . . change as a normal way of life requires that people find their stability and security not in specific organizational arrangements but in the culture and direction of the organization. It requires that they feel integrated with the whole rather than identified with the particular territory of the moment, since that is changeable (Kanter, 1983, p. 133).

Student affairs professionals in collaboration with other members of the campus community must take advantage of opportunities available to shape student cultures. Because student culture is complex, models of organizational change coupled with an informed approach to student culture are needed in order to effect cultural change.

Keep in mind, though, that cultural change is complex, time-consuming, and slow to demonstrate its effects. As a result, student affairs staff may be tempted to shift the focus of their energies from cultural change to other issues and concerns. Without purposeful planning, administrators may find their efforts haphazardly re-directed toward other activities. Long-term commitment to goals for cultural change as well as verbal and symbolic expressions focused on values and assumptions must be sustained long enough for the messages to be embraced by the community and incorporated into student culture. Said another way, the vision of what the college aspires to be must be consistently and continually expressed through symbols, language, physical artifacts, ceremonies, sagas, and other cultural artifacts over a long period of time, say five to eight years, before changes in student cultures will occur.

Activities

1. Using the mission of the institution as a point of reference, examine the cultural artifacts of the student culture and the student affairs culture. Do they reflect that mission? Are the messages communicated by cultural artifacts congruent with the mission and its underlying assumptions? Assuming these assumptions are com-

patible with the institutional mission, generate ideas on how these assumptions can be better displayed by cultural artifacts as well as more consistently reflected in routine administrative practice.

2. Examine videotapes of informal events and ceremonies (e.g., convocation, commencement) to identify cultural artifacts. Make a list of the messages *sent* and *received* during the event. Try this with a mixed group of students, faculty, and administrators to insure a wide variety of perspectives and points of view.

3. Analyze the criteria upon which leadership awards are chosen. Do all leaders on campus have a fair chance of meeting the criteria? Review the lists of winners for the past few years. Are women, students of color, and other under-represented groups included?

4. Periodically examine the underlying beliefs and assumptions of campus policies in staff meetings, during staff retreats, and through daily conversations. Student input about these issues can be extremely revealing and helpful.

5. Consider the age, race and ethnicity, sex, and sexual orientation of members of student advisory boards. Are the groups homogeneous or heterogeneous? What is the nature of the discussion in the group—consensus or divergent perspectives?

References

Astin, A.W. (1985). *Achieving educational excellence.* San Francisco: Jossey-Bass.

Bennett, W. (1984). *To reclaim a legacy.* Washington, D.C.: National Endowment for the Humanities.

Boyer, E.L. (1987) *College: The undergraduate experience in America.* New York: Harper & Row.

Bushnell, J. (1962). Student culture at Vassar. In N. Sanford (Ed.). *The American College* (pp. 489-514). New York: Wiley.

Clark, B. R. (1970). *The distinctive college: Antioch, Reed, and Swarthmore.* Chicago: Aldine.

Hodgkinson, H. (1984). *All one system: Demographics in education from kindergarten through graduate school.* Washington, D.C.: Institute for Educational Leadership, Inc.

Horowitz, H. L. (1987). *Campus life: Undergraduate cultures from the end of the eighteenth century to the present.* New York: Knopf.

Kanter, R.M. (1983). *The change masters: Innovation for productivity in the American corporation.* New York, NY: Simon and Schuster.

Kuh, G. D., & Lyons, J. W. (1990). Greek systems at "involving colleges": Lessons from the College Experiences Study. *NASPA Journal, 28,* 12.

Kuh, G. D., & MacKay, K. A. (1989). Beyond cultural awareness: Toward interactive pluralism. *Campus Activities Programming, 22* (4), 52–58.

Kuh, G. D., & Whitt, E. J. (1988). *The invisible tapestry: Culture in American colleges and universities.* ASHE-ERIC Higher Education Report, No. 1. Washington, D.C.: Association for the Study of Higher Education.

Lewis, A. (1980). The ritual process and community development. *Community Development Journal, 15,* 190–199.

Maisel, J. (1990). Social fraternity and sorority membership is not conducive to the educational process. *NASPA Journal, 28,* 8–12.

Manning, K. (1989). *Campus rituals and cultural meaning.* Bloomington, IN: Indiana University. Unpublished doctoral dissertation.

Marcus, G. (1988). Parody and the parodic in Polynesian cultural history. *Cultural Anthropology, 3,* 68–76.

McEwen, M., Roper, L., Bryant, D., & Langa, M. (1990). Incorporating the development of African American students into psychosocial theories of student development. *Journal of College Student Development, 31,* 429–436.

Moffatt, M. (1989). *Coming of age in New Jersey.* New Brunswick, NJ: Rutgers University Press.

Morgan, G. (1986). *Images of organizations.* Beverly Hills, CA: Sage.

Myerhoff, B. (1977). We don't wrap herring in the printed page:

Fusion, fictions and continuity in secular ritual. In S. Moore and B. Myerhoff (Eds.). *Secular ritual* (pp. 199–224). Amsterdam, Netherlands: Van Gorcum.

Myerhoff, B. (1984). A death in due time: Construction of self and culture in ritual drama. In J. MacAloon (Ed.), *Rite, drama, festival spectacle: Rehearsals toward a theory of cultural performance* (pp. 149–178). Philadelphia, PA: Institute for the Study of Human Issues.

Ortner, S. (1984). Theory in anthropology since the sixties. *Comparative Studies in Society and History, 2,* 126–166.

Rosner, J. (1990). Ways women lead. *Harvard Business Review,* November-December, 119–125.

Sanford, N. (1962). *The American College: A psychological and social interpretation of the higher learning.* New York: Wiley.

Sartorelli, M., & Fisher, V. (1992). Leadership programs: Building bridges between nontraditional and traditional students. *Campus Activities Programming, 24*(8), 41–48.

Siehl, C. (1985). After the founder: An opportunity to manage culture. In P. Frost, L. Moore, M. Louis, C. Lundberg, & J. Martin (Eds.), *Organizational culture* (pp. 125–140). Newbury Park, CA: Sage.

Turner, V. (1977a). Symbols in African ritual. In J. Dolgin, D. Kemnitzer and D. Schneider (Eds.), *Symbolic anthropology: A reader in the study of symbols and meanings* (pp. 183–194). New York: Columbia University Press.

Turner, V. (1977b). Variations on a theme of liminality. In S. Moore and B. Myerhoff (Eds.), *Secular ritual* (pp. 36–52). Amsterdam, Netherlands: Van Gorcum.

Van Maanen, J. (1984). Doing old things in new ways: The chains of socialization. In J. Bess (Ed.), *College and university organization: Insights from the behavioral sciences* (pp. 211–247). New York: New York University Press.

CHAPTER 7

Some Implications of Cultural Perspectives for Student Affairs

George D. Kuh

Things are not always what they seem. A college's culture, for example, is like an abalone shell. The shell looks different every time one looks at it because the shell is held a different way and the light strikes the shell from different angles (Frost, Moore, Louis, Lundberg & Martin, 1985). Another example of things not always being what they seem is the response one gets when seeking directions in the mountains of Peru. It is not uncommon to be told, "De aqui no se puede." Roughly translated that means, "you can't get there from here" (Wilkins & Patterson, 1986, p. 266). To Peruvians, this phrase does not mean that the destination is unattainable, but rather to "get there" one must negotiate numerous switchbacks and travel through one or more villages. "De aqui no se puede" acknowledges the many steps that must be taken before a challenging goal can be attained.

So it is with student affairs staff who desire to incorporate cultural perspectives into their work. They will face many challenges when attempting to encourage students to behave in ways more compatible with the institution's educational purposes. In the preceding chapter, Eaton and Manning offered ideas about how to go about shaping student culture. In this chapter, six suggestions are offered for how student affairs staff can use cultural perspectives in their daily routines.

SUGGESTIONS FOR USING
CULTURAL PERSPECTIVES

1. Think "culture."

To discover the influence of institutional policies and practices on student behavior, and to make the collegiate experience more humane and meaningful, one must *think* in cultural terms. That is, student affairs staff should actively seek out connections among events, actions, language, and physical environments. They also must examine their assumptions about human potential, teaching, and learning which influence their interpretations of why people think and behave the way they do at their institution.

At the core of an institution's culture are fundamental beliefs and assumptions about what is important. These shared ways of viewing institutional life become, in essence, a cognitive map, revealing to students, faculty, and others what the institution is like and how to get things done. In this sense, culture is what people believe about what works and what does not in their college. At the same time, the complicated set of content-bound, mutually shaping properties that make up an institution's culture, while seemingly stable over time, actually are constantly evolving.

As one begins to think in cultural terms, the cultural influences on behavior in various areas of the institution become more apparent. While many student affairs staff may not have at their disposal the results of a culture audit similar to that described in Chapter 5, participating in some of the activities suggested at the end of the preceding chapters will help one to identify artifacts, values, and— with assistance from colleagues—some of the core assumptions that drive institutional life.

In thinking about culture, student affairs staff should determine whether they have an obligation to address contradictions between what their institution *espouses* (says about itself in publications and public statements but may or may not actually do) and what seems to be *enacted* with regard to the philosophy, values, policies and practices (what people or the institution put into practice) described in Chapter 1. Espoused values may take the form of stated institutional aspirations, such as an announced commitment to health-enhancing behavior or to increasing the number of students and faculty from historically-underrepresented groups. When these goals do not materialize, the discrepancy between what the institution says about itself and what people observe and experience confuses and, at times, frustrates students and others.

2. Become an expert on the institution's culture.

By reading the institution's history and current publications, one can become familiar with some aspects of an institution's culture. Institutions of higher education are, in large measure, products of their histories. The purposes for which a college was founded, and the aspirations of the founding body, leave an indelible mark on an institution's character (Chaffee & Tierney, 1988; Clark, 1970; Frost et al., 1985; Kuh & Whitt, 1988). Therefore, knowledge of an institution's history is essential to understanding how a college or university became what it is at present and what makes it special.

The formal mission statement also should be reviewed. Keep in mind, however, that written mission statements may not accurately reflect the institution's "living mission." A living mission is what students, faculty, staff, graduates and others off the campus say their college does and aspires to be. When salient, a living mission guides the routines of institutional life and is congruent with what people actually do a good deal of the time (e.g., espoused goals are congruent with what actually takes place) (Kuh et al., 1991). By understanding a college's history and mission, one can relate the present to the past and maintain some degree of continuity among past, current, and future cohorts of student, faculty, and staff.

A student affairs division might devote an annual staff development session annually to examining present circumstances in the context of the institution's history. Another staff development activity might focus on trends in student behavior and attitudes distilled from the campus newspaper over the years. Brown-bag discussions with institutional historians (e.g., a long-time faculty member or perhaps a graduate from many decades ago) can help staff—particularly newcomers—better understand how events from the institution's past shaped current policies and practices.

As Manning points out in Chapter 2, ceremonies bring people together periodically. When used to educational advantage, ceremonies can address such important community challenges as mission clarification, affirmation of different groups of students, and collective mourning. Some years ago a university lost its president and two vice presidents in a plane crash. The emotional and organizational repercussions from that tragedy are still evident. Several staff and faculty members recently observed that the needed healing process following this loss was never completed, perhaps because their institution lacks forms of communal expression.

The status of various groups is often reflected in institutional traditions. Some traditions, such as hazing (the Rush period and Hell Week of fraternities, branding of African-American fraternity pledges) demean the worth and dignity of certain people. Traditions such as beauty contests, flying the Confederate flag (which many African-American students find offensive), and theme parties such as "Arabian Nights" or "Minstrel Shows" trivialize the experiences and backgrounds of women and racial and ethnic groups. Insidious stereotypes are perpetuated by slave auctions and pin-up calendars (Kuh et al., 1991). Student affairs staff should examine the messages communicated by such events along with the responses of various people to these messages. Such an analysis can contribute to a better understanding of the institution's character (Kuh, in press a) and to the development of strategies to establish an ethic of membership, a feeling that permeates the institution when all students, faculty, and staff are considered "full members" of the community and "belong" here (Kuh et al., 1991).

To affirm their achievements and heritage, students from historically underrepresented groups on occasion establish events for their particular group as part of the college's homecoming or commencement. Whether such events should be discouraged, or acknowledged as a "natural" phase in the evolution toward a multicultural campus, can only be determined on a case-by-case basis. In such instances, student affairs staff must be sensitive to the possibility that the expressed need for such events may reflect a growing frustration with an institution's inability or reluctance to embrace members of all groups as full members of the institution.

3. Teach culture.

There is no better way to expand one's knowledge about the institution's culture than by teaching it to others. Moreover, by transmitting those elements of the institutional culture that positively shape desired student behavior, one can be more intentional about reinforcing certain cultural properties over others.

Depending on the institution, from a quarter to more than a third of the students each year are newcomers. For this reason, it is inevitable that many will not understand what the institution expects of itself and of its students concerning a variety of practical issues, such as the use of alcohol, academic dishonesty, free speech, and multicultural influences. Assiduous efforts are required to teach newcomers about the institution's history, traditions, heroes and heroines, and other cultural artifacts that create appropriate expectations for student behavior and encourage learning and personal development. For example, at the University of Louisville, the statue of Supreme Court Justice Louis Brandeis is routinely pointed out to prospective students during campus tours, symbolizing that institution's commitment to racial equality (Strange, 1991).

Prior to their arrival, new students should be exposed to important institutional values and introduce them to their college's terms of endearment. For example, they should receive copies of the institutional history and other documents that offer insights into the philosophy of the institution. This way, the college establishes expectations and encourages positive behavior before the student culture, as was discussed in Chapter One, counters these messages with ideas that are incompatible with the institution's aims.

Another way to teach the culture of the campus is to tell stories about institutional events and the role of heroic figures. Stories communicate institutional values and aspirations. Anecdotes that convey examples of appropriate, successful behavior provide clues to students and staff about what is expected and what is valued. Events from the past can be described to illustrate to student groups why it is important for them to behave in certain ways.

Every institution has heroes and heroines in the student and faculty cultures whose exploits and achievements are typically far more compelling than what is written in a catalog or policy manual. At the University of California, Davis, each cohort of students learns from its predecessor about a former chancellor's concern that as the student body grows in numbers, "we must never lose the sense that we should care for one another." This aspiration has become part of the institution's philosophy; even though UC Davis now has more than 20,000 students, faculty often remark that the campus in many ways feels like a smaller institution.

Socialization is a double-edged sword. As we introduce new students and staff to institutional values, policies and practices may be unwittingly perpetuated that alienate certain people (e.g., members of historically underrepresented groups). Therefore, one must be very careful that when teaching culture, the lessons that are learned are those that reinforce inclusiveness. Deliberate decisions must be made about which institutional values merit support and which do not. I shall return to this point shortly.

4. Use symbolic action with intentionality.

Like it or not, the actions of student affairs professionals are always laden with symbolism. As institutional agents, student affairs staff cannot escape their responsibilities as role models. At the same time, any public act can be a teachable moment if used as an opportunity to tell students, colleagues, and others about the institution's values and what is expected of them.

Student affairs staff can induce students and faculty to come together in common cause when they use language that clearly and consistently communicates their institution's values, educational purposes, and expectations for student and faculty performance. How, to whom, and to what ends we speak carry messages about what, and who, is valued and how good learning communities ought to function.

Language gives clues to faculty, staff, and students about what is appropriate behavior, and who is welcome at the institution. Language also can empower and change the way people think about themselves and others. Thomas Ehrlich (1991), president of Indiana University (IU), with the enthusiastic support of the trustees, introduced a new term, "new majority students"; new majority students are traditional-age students of color or those who are older than 25, live off campus, work more than 20 hours a week, have families and attend college part time. Even though two-thirds of the students at seven of the eight IU campuses have for years met these criteria, the institution lacked a lexicon to acknowledge their presence and describe their experiences. New majority students now enjoy an enhanced status at Indiana University. Moreover, faculty, administrators, state legislators and others are changing the way they think about and work with students—a change in the culture if you will!

But language has inherent pitfalls. Words are easily misinterpreted or misused. Even something as important as establishing expectations for student performance is not without some risks, such as inducing stress. At Mount Holyoke College, for example, the phrase "uncommon women" represents high standards for student performance and an ideal toward which to strive. Students are encouraged to see themselves as "uncommon women" who can be anything they want to be. At the same time, the challenge to be "uncommon women" can create pressure to over-achieve, as well as to view some career and life choices—such as marriage and child-rearing—as unworthy (Whitt, 1991).

Different groups within the institution may sometimes develop their own language. For example, even within the "student affairs rainforest" (Schroeder, Nicholls & Kuh, 1983), the language spoken by residence life staff differs somewhat from that used in financial aids and career planning. In addition, every college has a "shadow side," unsavory practices or norms that over time become a part of the everyday life of the institution; this shadow side of a college's culture is often revealed through its language. For example, speeches and other public statements by institutional leaders can be used as a barometer of the institution's commitment to multiculturalism. Such statements, while important, may become counterproductive if the everyday language and behavior of the campus ignores members of historically-underrepresented groups, makes them invisible, or degrades them (Kuh et al., 1991). If terms of disrespect or lack of respect are used frequently, student affairs staff must challenge such language and substitute in their place terms of inclusion and respect so that people are not kept invisible or in any way demeaned.

Often student affairs staff, particularly young professionals, find it awkward to use the symbolic power of language in the service of institutional values and aspirations. Learning how to speak in public and knowing when and how to invoke history, institutional symbols, and heroes and heroines to underscore the importance of certain behaviors, are important skills to cultivate.

5. Never underestimate the tenacity of culture.

Although the properties that make up an institution's culture are constantly evolving, many of the institution's core assumptions about human nature are deeply rooted. For this reason, student affairs staff must be cautious in celebrating what appears to be success in modifying traditions and practices that are antithetical to the institution's educational aims. Just when it appears as if the behavior of a countercultural group of students has been stamped out, such as a sexist tradition sponsored by a social group, next year's membership, or another group, introduces a similar event.

That this happens should not be surprising because the underlying assumptions about certain groups of people at the core of the college's culture can be expected to surface in some form. Make no mistake, modifying the most debilitating aspects of a culture demands constant and continuous attention over more than a few years.

In most colleges and universities, open, meaningful discussion of the differences between espoused and enacted preferences and beliefs is difficult to realize (Kuh in press a). This sort of discussion is well illustrated by the unsuccessful efforts to modify certain practices of fraternities and sororities, such as hazing and hazardous use of alcohol (Arnold & Kuh, 1992). Cultural change is more amenable to persuasion rather than edict; indeed, in times of crisis, the tacit assumptions that comprise the "hidden core" (Schein, 1985) of collegiate cultures tend to come to the surface. While this makes it easier for insiders and outsiders to identify these assumptions, it also makes them more difficult to change as people will cling more tenaciously to these fundamental beliefs (Wilkins, 1989).

As with dysfunctional families, many institutions have pervasive norms that discourage discussion of differences in most forums with the possible exception of some classes. That is, some problems and issues exist (e.g., racism, homophobia) that cannot be dealt with openly because strong cultural taboos prevent people from talking about them or even publically acknowledging their existence (Kuh, in press a). In some instances, these norms either no longer serve the purposes for which they were intended or persist for reasons other than those used to establish the practice.

Krefting and Frost (1985) suggested that trying to change culture is similar to:

"the surfer who must ride a wave to its conclusion, always facing the risks of unexpected swirls from the depths beneath the wave as well as the unpredictable air movements on and above the surface. In fact, it is likely that changes of high intensity will require the manager to ride out a succession of waves, falling off some and striving to remain secure on others (p. 157)

To be sure, as agents of the institution, student affairs staff have a responsibility to influence the campus culture in ways that are compatible with attaining the institution's purposes. At the same time, one must recognize that cultural change is a long, difficult process. The dominant will of a group of people does not guarantee that culture will change. By the same token, living and working in the institutional context also influences our own behavior in ways that we are cognizant of as well as in ways to which we may be oblivious.

6. Clarify and hold fast to the vision.

In the final analysis, a college or university is what its faculty, graduates, trustees, and others believe it is (Wilkins, 1989). In essence, to nurture an educationally purposeful culture, students, faculty, staff, graduates and others must have faith in the ability of their college to prosper, develop, mature and remain viable. People must have faith in their own ability to successfully respond to the challenges facing their institution. If student affairs professionals are to nurture such faith in students and their faculty and staff colleagues, they must trust them and exhibit a fundamental fairness in carrying out their leadership roles. Furthermore, student affairs professionals must display integrity through their everyday actions by challenging colleagues who do not display integrity to modify their behavior or encourage them to seek employment elsewhere.

For people to believe in their college, a vision is needed of what the college is and can become. The student affairs culture is deeply rooted in commitments and values affirmed over the past 50 years (American Council on Education, 1937, 1949; National Association of Student Personnel Administrators, 1987). Any vision developed by the student affairs division about how the campus can enhance student learning and personal development must be compatible with certain principles (e.g., helping students develop life skills and values strongly held by the institution) and with the institution's mission, educational purposes, and philosophy. Student affairs staff must first discover the mission of their college before they can articulate it and—through their behavior—be a living symbol of the mission of their institution (Kuh & Schuh, 1991; Kuh et al., 1991). For those who wish to use culture in their work, knowing and living the mission of the institution is a critical requirement.

Using cultural perspectives to educational advantage requires a vision of what the institution will look like when students take

responsibility for their learning and actively engage in education-
ally-purposeful activities outside the classroom. The amount of
attention students devote to learning is, in part, a function of the
degree to which their institution values learning. Senior student
affairs professionals can create such a shared reality. The long tenure of some chief student affairs officers, such as James Lyons at
Stanford University and James Rhatigan at Wichita State University, leave an imprint on how student affairs is viewed by faculty,
what the student affairs division considers important, and how
business is to be conducted. Student affairs professionals who have
had a profound, positive impact on their campuses share certain
characteristics: they are willing to get involved with students, develop a deep affective commitment to their institution, and challenge policies and practices that create unwanted distinctions among
groups of people.

In partnership with other institutional leaders, senior student
affairs staff must be "keepers of the vision" who are committed to
sustaining precious institutional values while simultaneously challenging policies and practices that either become obstacles to student learning and personal development or relegate certain groups
of students to second class citizenry. Included in such a vision is
what sort of education the institution should provide its students,
what behaviors are expected from students, and what qualities characterize a healthy and effective academic community. In all actions,
uphold the idealized version of the institutional values. The role of
the chief student affairs officer and other senior student affairs staff
is to persuade faculty, students and others that the vision has merit,
keep people focused on this vision, and expend the effort necessary to maintaining a commitment to attain the vision.

CONCLUDING THOUGHTS

This book is not the final word on using cultural perspectives in
student affairs. Discovering how an institution's culture and subcultures influence student behavior is an evolutionary process. The
contributors will be satisfied if this volume encourages student
affairs professionals to contribute to a dialogue on their campus
about how their institution's cultures influence student learning and
personal development. In addition, we hope that more student affairs professionals, in partnership with students and faculty col-

leagues, begin to experiment with cultural perspectives in examining institutional problems and challenges.

To have a positive impact on the quality of student life, sustained research efforts are needed by scholars and practitioners using culture as a frame of reference. Much more empirical work is needed on student subcultures and how institutional culture influences student expectations, attitudes, and behavior. A partial list of relevant issues that can be illuminated using cultural perspectives includes examinations of:

(a) conditions associated with hazardous use of alcohol and other controlled substances by certain subgroups and the institutional philosophies, policies, and practices that encourage health-enhancing behavior on the part of students, faculty and others (Kuh, 1990, in press b);

(b) socialization of newcomers—new staff, faculty, and students—to positive institutional values;

(c) successful efforts to modify the institution's culture and various campus subcultures to enhance a sense of campus community; and

(d) strategies for reducing the disparity between espoused institutional values and aspirations for multiculturalism and enacted institutional policies and practices.

The methods to "discover" the cultural properties of a college or university are many and varied. Some believe quantitative methods such as surveys and questionnaires can be used; others believe quantitative methods are anathema to the symbolic, tacit features of culture. The resurgence of interest in studying collegiate cultures is propitious. There is an increased acceptance of naturalistic or qualitative methods in many areas of social science that value and validate subjective interpretation of contexts, events, behaviors and so on (Kuh, 1991; Kuh & Andreas, 1991; Kuh, Whitt & Shedd, 1987). Understanding how such subjective elements of institutional life contribute to creating a sense of community on campus is critical to the vitality of American higher education. The position advocated here is that only qualitative methods such as interviews and observations can accurately discover and describe some of the less visible aspects of culture such as values and beliefs.

According to Pascarella and Terenzini (1991), the contextual conditions of a campus (an institution's cultures if you will!) are more important to student learning than organizational and programmatic variables. In other words, reorganizing the division of student affairs, or adding student affairs programs, may not make much of a difference in what or how much the majority of students learn. More important to enhancing the impact of college is complementarity among institutional values, policies, and practices that is a hallmark of a coherent, integrated undergraduate experience. A key task for institutional agents, then, is to discover how their institution's culture promotes or inhibits students' engagement with learning and personal development opportunities. We challenge student affairs professionals to become adept at thinking in cultural terms and to exert leadership on their campus in examining how their institution's cultures can be shaped to enhance student learning and personal development.

REFERENCES

American Council on Education (1937). *The student personnel point of view.* Washington, D.C.: American Council on Education.

American Council on Education (1949). *The student personnel point of view.* Washington, D.C.: American Council on Education.

Arnold, J.C., & Kuh, G.D. (1992). *Brotherhood and the bottle: A cultural analysis of the role of alcohol in fraternities.* Bloomington, IN: The Center for the Study of the College Fraternity.

Chaffee, E.E., & Tierney, W.G. (1988). *Collegiate culture and leadership strategy.* New York: American Council on Education and Macmillan.

Clark, B.R. (1970). *The distinctive college: Reed, Antioch, and Swarthmore.* Chicago: Aldine.

Ehrlich, T. (1991). *Our university in the state: Educating the new majority.* Bloomington, IN: Indiana University.

Frost, P.J., Moore, L.F., Louis, M.R., Lundberg, C.C., & Martin, J. (1985). An allegorical view of organizational culture. In P.J. Frost, L.F. Moore, M.R. Louis, C.C. Lundberg, and J. Martin, (Eds.), *Organizational culture* (pp. 13–23). Beverly Hills, CA: Sage.

Krefting, L.A., & Frost, P.J. (1985). Untangling webs, surfing waves, and wildcatting: A multiple metaphor perspective on managing organizational culture. In P. Frost, L. Moore, M. Louis, C. Lundberg, & J. Martin (Eds.), *Organizational culture* (pp. 155–168). Beverly Hills, CA: Sage.

Kuh, G.D. (1990). Assessing student culture. In W. G. Tierney (Ed.), *Assessing academic climates and cultures, New Directions for Institutional Research*, No. 68 (pp. 47–60). San Francisco: Jossey-Bass.

Kuh, G.D. (1991). Rethinking research in student affairs. In K. Beeler and D. Hunter (Eds.), *Puzzles and pieces in wonderland: The promise and practice of student affairs research* (pp. 55-79). Washington, D.C.: National Association of Student Personnel Administrators.

Kuh, G.D. (1993). Appraising the character of a college. *Journal of Counseling and Development, 71.* (a)

Kuh, G.D. (in press). What do we know about the influence of college environments on student drinking? In G. Gonzalez and V. Veltri (Eds.), *Implications of research and policy for alcohol and other drug programs on college campuses.* Washington, D.C.: National Association of Student Personnel Administrators. (b)

Kuh, G.D., & Andreas, R.E. (1991). It's about time: Using qualitative research methods in student affairs. *Journal of College Student Development, 32,* 397–405.

Kuh, G.D., & Schuh, J.H. (Eds.). (1991). *The role and contributions of student affairs in Involving Colleges.* Washington, D.C.: National Association of Student Personnel Administrators.

Kuh, G.D., Schuh, J.H., Whitt, E.J., Andreas, R.E., Lyons, J.W., Strange, C.C., Krehbiel, L.E., & MacKay, K.A. (1991). *Involving colleges: Successful approaches to fostering student learning and development outside the classroom.* San Francisco: Jossey-Bass.

Kuh, G.D., & Whitt, E.J. (1988). *The invisible tapestry: Culture in American colleges and universities.* ASHE-ERIC Higher Education Report, No. 1. Washington, D.C.: American Association for Higher Education.

Kuh, G.D., Whitt, E.J., & Shedd, J. (1987). *Student affairs, 2001: A paradigmatic odyssey.* Alexandria, VA: ACPA Media.

National Association of Student Personnel Administrators (1987). *A perspective on student affairs.* Washington, D.C.: National Association of Student Personnel Administrators.

Pascarella, E.T., & Terenzini, P.T. (1991). *How college affects students.* San Francisco: Jossey-Bass.

Schein, E.H. (1985). *Organizational culture and leadership.* San Francisco: Jossey-Bass.

Schroeder, C.C., Nicholls, G.M., & Kuh, G.D. (1983). Exploring the "rain-forest: Testing assumptions and taking risks. In G. Kuh (Ed.), *Understanding student affairs organizations, New Directions for Student Services*, No. 23 (pp. 51-65). San Francisco: Jossey-Bass.

Strange, C.C. (1991). Emergence of a metroversity: The University of Louisville case. In G. Kuh and J. Schuh (Eds.), *The role and contributions of student affairs in Involving Colleges* (pp. 72–89). Washington, D.C.: National Association of Student Personnel Administrators.

Whitt, E. J. (1991). A community of women empowering women: Mount Holyoke College. In G. Kuh and J. Schuh (Eds.), *The role and contributions of student affairs in Involving Colleges* (pp. 120–143). Washington, D.C.: National Association of Student Personnel Administrators.

Wilkins, A.L. (1989). *Developing corporate character: How to successfully change an organization without destroying it.* San Francisco: Jossey-Bass.

Wilkins, A.L., & Patterson, K.J. (1986). You can't get there from here: What will make culture-change projects fail. In R. Kilmann, M. Saxton, R. Serpa and Associates (Eds.), *Gaining control of the corporate culture* (pp. 262–291). San Francisco: Jossey-Bass.